MW00572444

Corolla's

WILD

HORSES

Corolla's
WILD
HORSES

A HISTORY

JEFF HAMPTON

Foreword by Meg Puckett, herd manager for the Corolla Wild Horse Fund

THE
History
PRESS

Published by The History Press
Charleston, SC
www.historypress.com

Copyright © 2023 by Jeff Hampton
All rights reserved

First published 2023

Manufactured in the United States

ISBN 9781467153546

Library of Congress Control Number: 2022950052

Notice: The information in this book is true and complete to the best of our knowledge. It is offered without guarantee on the part of the author or The History Press. The author and The History Press disclaim all liability in connection with the use of this book.

All rights reserved. No part of this book may be reproduced or transmitted in any form whatsoever without prior written permission from the publisher except in the case of brief quotations embodied in critical articles and reviews.

Contents

Foreword, by Meg Puckett   7
Acknowledgements   9

1. Star the Magnificent Stallion   11
2. Spanish Mustangs or Banker Ponies   21
3. Little Red Man Can't Be Fenced In   29
4. Big Crowds Want to See Wild Horses   42
5. How Many Horses Are Too Many?   47
6. A Killer Shoots Them Down   51
7. Another Fence and More Laws Protect the Herd   55
8. McCalpin Goes to Washington   66
9. Briars Taste Good   69
10. Adopt a Horse   77
11. Ready to Rumble   81
12. A Refuge for Ailing and Wayward Horses   84
13. It's All in the Genes   90
14. Amadeo   94
15. Roamer   97
16. Raymond the Mule   103
17. Still Trying to Save Horses   106
18. Raising Money   113

Contents

Notes 117

Index 123

About the Author 125

Foreword

The wild Banker ponies of Corolla are an intrinsic part of our Outer Banks history, the same as pirates, ghost ships and disappearing colonists. For the last five hundred years, they have managed to not just survive on this inhospitable spit of land but thrive. They are as much a part of our landscape as the dunes and the sea oats, and it's hard to imagine an Outer Banks without wild ponies roaming freely among the live oaks.

But as times change, so does the need for more protection, more advocacy and a better understanding of just what makes these horses tick. The more we learn about them, the better equipped we are to shape a future for them here that will ensure their survival for another five centuries. This means understanding how they utilize their environment, from what they eat to how they traverse the habitat. It means studying their DNA to identify genetic anomalies and learn more about the science behind survival. It means working closely with our community—with local, state and federal governments; with business and property owners; and with the hundreds of thousands of yearly visitors—to make sure we are all playing an active role in their protection.

It also means preserving and sharing their history, because that history is *our* history.

The Bankers are a cultural treasure, and their story—past, present and future—is one that deserves to be told in a way that acknowledges the legends and lore, the true history, the science and the people who have worked tirelessly over the decades to protect them, care for them and be a voice for them. In this book, Jeff has done all of that. He presents a comprehensive, well-researched, balanced look at everything that makes these horses so special and so worth saving. It is an invaluable resource that is not only preserving history but also providing an updated overview of the horses' biology, their ecological impact and current management practices.

—Meg Puckett
herd manager, Corolla Wild Horse Fund

ACKNOWLEDGEMENTS

I want to thank current and former directors and volunteers of Corolla Wild Horse Fund, including Meg Puckett, Karen McCalpin, Donna Snow, Lloyd Childers and Dru Hodges. Their input was invaluable. I am grateful to the photographers who contributed to this book, including Drew Wilson, Erin Millar, Meg Puckett and Kaye Beasely, whose pictures are attributed to Currituck County. My wife, Irene, was immensely helpful in editing the book and giving me encouragement.

Chapter 1

STAR THE MAGNIFICENT STALLION

I n the early 1980s, a muscled black stallion with attitude galloped and grazed among the sandy roads of the undeveloped village of Corolla. The few people who lived on these remote Currituck County barrier islands called him Star for the white patch on his forehead. Star was one of Corolla's wild horses descended from Banker ponies that have lived on the Outer Banks for five centuries. He was among the first to gain fame beyond the Currituck Outer Banks. He dominated other stallions and fiercely protected his harem of mares.[1] Those who saw him described him as magnificent.

Star roamed Corolla as a young horse before the village grew into a tourist attraction with expansive neighborhoods of massive homes. He was there when the first paved road came through. He saw a major transition from quiet community to bustling beach town—a threat that he could not know at the time was more dangerous to him and his herd than any storm or rival stallion. His eyes were well spaced on a broad forehead. His tail was set low on a muscled back end, giving him extra power for quick takeoffs and sudden bursts of speed. The strong and durable characteristics are common in these horses.

Following Star is a long line of equine characters who have lived over the last forty years renowned for their individual personalities, goofiness, fortitude, fierceness, friendliness and tragic endings. More than one hundred wild horses now live on about twelve thousand acres of beaches, maritime forests, meadows and marshes. Some of that acreage is fenced within the

Star the stallion was among the first of the Corolla wild horses to become widely known. *Drew Wilson.*

Currituck National Wildlife Refuge. Roughly eight hundred homes are clustered in communities. The horses can die from many causes, man-made and natural. In recent decades, people have helped watch over them and saved them. At the same time, humans have caused their deaths in some cases. Leaders of the Corolla Wild Horse Fund have defended horses in the streets, herded them to safety, delivered them from injuries, promoted them to the public and kept watch over them from people who mistreated them accidentally or on purpose. Herd managers eventually found a way to better protect them in a more isolated part of the Outer Banks north of Corolla by fencing them within their habitat and away from paved highways and the heaviest development.

Wild horse officials worked with national equine organizations to get the herd listed as rare, authentic Spanish mustangs, although that designation is disputed. They spoke before lawmakers in Washington, D.C., in an effort to expand the herd size for its health and protection from extinction. They became public relations specialists, telling the wild horse story almost daily on social media. The fame of Corolla's wild horses has spread across the world. People love the romance of them still roaming free on a barrier island. Thousands want to see them and take photographs of them. T-shirts, photographs, books, posters, caps and cups all are big sellers. Some want to feed them and get close enough to touch them, both dangerous and illegal practices.

Any number of alarming threats could decimate the herd in a short time despite the cadre of caretakers working day and night to preserve them. Death can come to individual horses from a wide range of sources, including an overflow of unhealthy garbage at rental cottages to deadly illnesses brought on by pests and bacteria thriving in their drinking water after a trend of warmer winters. Years ago, several horses were purposely shot dead. The killings were never solved even after an extensive investigation. Horses are still struck and killed on the beach. A young horse died in 2020 after it swallowed an apple fed to him by a tourist. Wild horses are not accustomed to the same food as domestic horses. The destructive clashes, unintended or intentional, continue on, coming from different sources, constantly keeping managers on their guard. Yet the herd thrives within these precarious circumstances.

One caretaker recorded that she said prayers every night for the safety of the horses, that nothing tragic would happen while she slept. Many of those prayers were for Star. In the late 1980s, Star appeared daily in the Corolla village leading his group of mares, at times grazing under the lighthouse near the deteriorating keepers' houses or wandering over the grounds of the gray, aging Whalehead Club. Locals had to watch where they stepped to avoid a fresh pile of horse dung at their front step or even on the porch. The horses roamed where they wanted, in and out of the village populated by a few homes, a schoolhouse and a church. The only commercial development in Corolla was a small complex north of the lighthouse that included the Winks general store, the post office and a real estate office. People woke in the morning to see them grazing in their yards. Cars on the sandy roads stopped when horses passed by, as they would for a group of schoolchildren. Developments like Whalehead Beach, Ocean Hill and Corolla Village were approved and platted in the 1970s. A few dozen homes had gone up within them, and the human population slowly grew. Realtor Kay Cole remembers arriving in 1983 and becoming only the sixteenth person registered to vote in Corolla. Year-round residents numbered fewer than forty.[2]

Developers put up a gate in the late 1970s at the end of the paved road just north of Duck. Only property owners and guests could pass through on the drive to Corolla. Commercial fishermen were allowed through if they showed their gear. Some people threw fishing equipment in their trucks just to get by the gate. Local and state officials wanted to remove the gate to allow full public access to Corolla.

Former Currituck County commissioner Wilson Snowden remembered how he, state representative Vernon James and other elected officials rode on NC 12 on a bus with a state trooper accompanying them. It was November 1984. Once at the gate, the trooper, with state authority, told the guard to exit the gatehouse before he pushed it over on its side. That's when the North Carolina Department of Transportation took over the road. It was about then that the road into Corolla was paved, but the onrush of traffic didn't happen until the following spring as the new tourist season began. Development boomed after that, and life changed for the horses, which were accustomed to traveling where they wished without much danger. With the paved road came more housing and business construction. Developers put in sod with beautiful, tender green grass and dug drainage ponds. The horses could enjoy a lush meal at the ready and something to drink as well. Traffic would become a deadly menace to the horses after centuries of surviving the Outer Banks elements. Suddenly, literally overnight, they were in danger of extinction in the village.

The early carnage was shocking. In August 1989, eight horses were killed on NC 12 within days of each other. A month-old colt was killed and then another foal days later.[3] Shortly after that, three pregnant mares were struck and killed in an accident that happened after dark. The death toll included the unborn foals. Emergency responders arrived to find mares dead in the road with blood covering the pavement. It was a horrible scene. One of the mares was found the next day dying in the woods and had to be euthanized. The vehicle that hit the horses was traveling more than sixty miles per hour in a thirty-five-mile-per-hour zone. Their deaths appalled the community, who could not help but take action. About seventy people met at the firehouse in Corolla to debate the problem. Soon afterward, a dedicated group of locals organized themselves into the Corolla Wild Horse Fund, led by Rowena Dorman, Dru Hodges, Debbie Westner and Jane Webster. The group would fall under the auspices of the nonprofit Outer Banks Conservationists, which had formed in 1980 to save the Currituck Beach Lighthouse and the keepers' houses in Corolla.

Organizers of the fund quickly learned the massive attraction of the wild horses and that managing the herd would be a big job. Detractors dismissed their efforts trying to preserve the horses, contending these were domestic animals that adapted to their circumstances and became feral. They questioned the sentimentality and necessity of giving them names. Herd advocates believed every horse had its own personality and each deserved to be individualized. Names quickly helped them know what each horse

Wild horses walking on busy NC 12 in Corolla before the fence was built in the early 1990s. *Drew Wilson.*

was doing and the behavior to expect in case of clashes with people. Names helped them keep track of the population and health of the herd. The women sometimes questioned themselves on whether they were on the fringe of insanity putting so much time and effort into the horses. But as the popularity of the horses grew, so did their support at high levels in state and federal government. After a year of hard work, successes and heartaches, in 1990 horse fund president Debbie Westner received congratulatory letters from state and national elected officials, including state senator Marc Basnight, Secretary of State Rufus L. Edmisten and U.S. senator Terry Sanford.

"I am confident that the historic Spanish Mustangs are going to survive in Currituck County because of your good labors and the sacrifices of the many others who have had a hand in helping you,'" said a letter from Sanford. In June 1995, the North Carolina Department of Cultural Resources issued a proclamation that in part said, "The Corolla Wild Horses are one of the most significant historic and cultural resources of the coastal area."[4]

Collisions between cars and horses continued despite the efforts of the horse fund volunteers. Corolla bustled with vehicles driven by people not accustomed to encountering wild horses darting across the road. The horses were unaware of the dangers posed by the influx of people and commerce. Twenty horses were killed on the highway between 1985 and 1995, according to media reports at the time. There was a real fear that the herd could disappear in a hurry. Horses came to associate the road and vehicles with food. People would stop and feed them from their car windows.

Star was the wildest and boldest of them all yet somehow managed to escape a collision for seven years after the road was opened to the public. He often stood regally on the top of a dune watching over the others of his harem as they grazed, almost showing off his prowess and superiority among other wild stallions. Dru Hodges remembers seeing Star trot by her kitchen window. He stopped at the top of a dune silhouetted against the rising sun behind him. She still remembers the amazing image almost four decades later.

"He knew he was something else," Hodges recalled.

Hodges worked full time in the Currituck County planning office in Corolla, volunteered as an emergency medical technician, raised her family and still found time to serve as secretary of the wild horse organization. She wants the epitaph on her gravestone to read, "I can't imagine a heaven without horses." She praised the efforts of the others she worked with, calling them "relentless" in the cause.

Star's harem of six to eight horses was among about two dozen roaming the village of Corolla. Star was literally a stud among stallions, mating with mares and producing foals prolifically, according to a genealogy generated by herd managers. Star sired or is an ancestor of many of the herd still roaming the banks today. He mated with a pretty mare named Baygirl and sired Butterscotch in 1981, to be followed by eight others in the next few years, including Risky, Baby Dumpling, Flicka and Ms. Tina. Over the years, Star also mated with his own offspring, producing sixteen other foals over nine years. In 1987, he sired a colt named Midnight that would prove to be a constant challenger to him.

Midnight was a proud horse like his father, and their relationship was the classic calamity of a stubborn father and a headstrong son. Star and Midnight battled often over control of the herd, rearing, kicking and biting as stallions had done on these banks for generations. Midnight carried a scar over his nose, likely from one of those fights.

The old man won every time. Midnight had no offspring for his first few years as he matured and learned from his dominating father how a stallion kept control. Midnight eventually left Corolla village to go up to the north beaches and find his own way. He was gone for months before returning to the village with a mare named Molly. She was a bay with a black mane and tail and black-colored lower legs. She was high ranking in Midnight's harem. She did not like to be bossed around, according to a description of her written at the time. It was like Midnight came back to dare his father to take this one away. He would be the stallion of his own harem in his home territory despite Star. The fighting between the two was so frequent that in the summer of 1990, herd managers wanted to neuter one of them and asked for a variance in county law that prohibited harming or handling the horses. A neutered horse would be much less likely to fight. The Currituck County Board of Commissioners decided against the change, believing it would bring on the wrath of animal protection groups.[5]

Midnight and Molly sired a foal named M&M in 1990. But as had happened so many times before, Star proved he was in charge and the stronger stallion. He battled Midnight over Molly and took the attractive mare away from his feisty son. In June 1991, Molly gave birth to Star's last colt. He was named Two Socks for white coloring on his lower hind legs.[6] As Two Socks grew, he showed he was not respectful to the dominant stallions and often got kicked out of the harem. He would never know his father, Star. He was born a month too late. About the same time, Star's longtime mare Baygirl gave birth to Ms. Tina, a chestnut named for her unruly mane similar to the hair of singer Tina Turner. She would be the last filly sired by Star.

On the morning of May 11, 1991, Star and Midnight were fighting again near the Monteray Shores neighborhood. Once again, Star got the best of his son and chased him from his harem at nearly full speed. The pursuit took the horses across NC 12, where traffic was so often heavy. Midnight bolted across without incident, but Star ran into a vehicle at nearly full speed and was killed. The driver was not at fault. He had braked to let the horses pass. There was no avoiding it, according to the State Highway Patrol at the time.[7] Stallions in the middle of a fight and subsequent chase of a challenger focus

People watching a wild foal near the Currituck lighthouse. *Drew Wilson.*

on nothing else. Star could see only his nemesis ahead of him and did not see the vehicle. That unfiltered sense of survival of the most dominant, bred into him over centuries, led to his death.

It was a shock to the people who had attempted to preserve the small herd living in the village from the onslaught of traffic and development. The passing of the beautiful black stallion with the symmetrical white patch on his forehead devastated the few people living year-round in Corolla. Many cried when they heard the news. Star was not the first horse killed by a vehicle, but it was the single most traumatic to those who loved the horses. After Star's untimely death, fundraising grew, and more people joined the wild horse organization. Corolla Wild Horse Fund membership grew quickly from a handful of people around Corolla to hundreds, including many from outside the area. The accident spurred an even greater effort to protect the Corolla wild horses.

In June 1991, the month after Star's death, *Outer Banks Magazine* published a photo of him posing like a war horse with an arched neck and legs stepping high in the sand. Many months earlier, *The Virginian-Pilot* photographer Drew Wilson had snapped the photo while on assignment with a reporter doing a story on the wild horses.[8] Wilson remembers he found a small herd on the beach and took photos of them, including the lead stallion, who happened to be Star. The stallion was at the edge of the surf with the ocean sparkling behind him. Wilson caught him in the photo with a front leg up and his neck arched as if he were prancing. His black body contrasted perfectly in front of the water. The scene could not have been more idyllic for a wild horse picture.

The newspaper story ran immediately after the photo assignment. As beautiful as the photo was, it was not selected to run in the paper. Wilson was contacted later to see what photos he had of wild horses to run with a story in the *Outer Banks Magazine*. The editor chose the unpublished photo of Star by the water for the cover. Publications like that take much more lead time than a news story. Weeks before the magazine hit the stands, Star was killed. It was too late to change plans for the cover photo. The magazine editor decided to make Star's death as positive as possible. The cover photo would be made into a poster and offered for sale. All the proceeds would go to the Corolla Wild Horse Fund. The magazine cover of Star in that prancing pose made into a poster immediately became a bestseller.[9] Horse lovers across America bought it, and the image became representative of Corolla's wild horses. That poster still hangs on the wall of the Corolla Wild Horse Fund headquarters and gift shop in the center of the village. It was the inspiration for all sorts of artwork, including quilts, paintings, wood carvings and T-shirts. The image is legendary.

Ten-year-old Meg Puckett got the poster for Christmas. She placed it on her bedroom wall, always seeing it when she rose in the morning and when she retired at night. Puckett would become herd manager of the wild horses in 2016 and still was as of this writing. The poster of Star inspired her to want to work with Corolla's wild horses one day. Star's poster still hangs in her home.[10] Star was buried near where he was killed in a vacant right-of-way for power lines. A plaque commemorating him stands on a post on the east side of the Currituck Beach Lighthouse shaded by a canopy of live oaks and not easily seen by the hundreds of visitors who climb the beacon daily.

The plaque features a representation of the image of Star that ran on the magazine cover and became the famous poster. The photo might be the most iconic of all the thousands taken of the Corolla wild horses.

The metal plate with raised lettering reads:

In Memory of Star, The Majestic Black Stallion of the Corolla Wild Horses In his innocence, he respected and tolerated man. He protected his own, but even with his wild wisdom, he could not protect himself. Over the years, Star saw eight of his mares and seven foals killed by vehicles. Star was killed May 11, 1991. His memory will remain forever with the shifting sands of Corolla.

Chapter 2

SPANISH MUSTANGS

OR BANKER PONIES

As gentle and relatively small as they are today, Corolla wild horses could descend in part from mounts used by fierce warriors. Islamic fighters, including Arabs and Moors from North Africa, rode their fast, durable horses to conquer a land that is modern-day Spain early in the eighth century. According to the book *The Horse of the Americas* by Robert Denhardt, the horses of the Outer Banks could have lines going back to a single famous stallion named Guzman taken to what became Spain by the king of Morocco to fight in those battles.[11] Barb or Berber horses are believed to be a blend of the horses used by the Moors from the Barbary Coast in North Africa and horses indigenous to the Iberian Peninsula.[12] The warriors known as Moors remained in power for nearly eight hundred years until the Spanish vanquished them hundreds of years later. These horses from the Barbary Coast and other breeds were transported to the New World.

It is widely believed that in 1493, Christopher Columbus brought horses to the Americas that were the first since prehistoric equines went extinct.[13] Some archaeological and oral history evidence exists that horses lived in the Americas before Columbus arrived.[14] The horses were eventually bred on ranches that spread throughout South and Central America.[15] Horses were loaded on ships and unloaded to land using a system of ropes attached to a strap fixed under their bellies.[16] Afterward, Columbus and others brought more horses and quickly set up breeding ranches in Hispaniola and South America, Denhardt wrote.

By the end of the 1600s, wild horses roamed large areas of the United States and helped mobilize Native American tribes.[17] Some groups came to live along the Eastern Seaboard of the United States. No one knows exactly how the Banker horses came to be roaming the North Carolina Outer Banks, but there are theories.

They may have spread into North America through trade from the ranches and colonization from South America. Spanish and English explorers may have left horses along the coast. The earliest Spanish expedition that possibly ventured into coastal states including North Carolina was looking for Native slaves in the 1520s.[18] Lucas Vázquez de Ayllón attempted to settle an area that may have been in the Cape Fear region in the 1520s. He brought eighty-nine horses with him. The settlement failed after many of the people sickened and died, including de Ayllón. A few survivors sailed back to Hispaniola, leaving behind their herds of livestock.[19]

Horses could have come ashore after shipwrecks. Thousands of ships have wrecked off the coast known as the Graveyard of the Atlantic. It is possible many English and Spanish ships went down, losing supplies and livestock, including horses. In June 1585, the English ship the *Tiger*, part of the Walter Raleigh expeditions to the North Carolina coast, ran aground off Ocracoke. It was carrying supplies and livestock, including horses. It took on enough water to ruin supplies, and historians believe the crew may have sent some of the horses and other animals overboard to lighten the load.[20] The horses multiplied into herds along the North Carolina coast from Shackleford Banks to Ocracoke to Corolla. The Corolla horses have bloodlines that closely match the breeds from South America and Mexico.[21]

Adventurers recorded seeing wild horses on North Carolina's coast over the next centuries. John Lawson wrote about them in 1709, saying, "The horses are well-shaped and swift. The best of them would sell for ten or twelve pounds in England. They prove excellent drudges, and will travel incredible journeys."[22]

In 1775, a sixteen-year-old girl named Betsy Dowdy rode one of the wild horses of the Currituck Outer Banks to help turn the tide of a Revolutionary War conflict. It was the Outer Banks version of Paul Revere's ride, but it was fraught with more danger from the elements. The legend is told in the 1901 book *Grandfather's Tales of North Carolina* by Richard B. Creecy. The veracity of the story has been questioned, but it remains a favorite. The Elizabeth City chapter of the Daughters of the American Revolution named their group in honor of Betsy Dowdy in 1937. The story begins with Lord Dunmore, royal governor of the Province of

Virginia, who administered the colony in the king's name. It was about this time that Patrick Henry declared in a Richmond speech, "Give me liberty or give me death." Virginians organized into an armed resistance against Dunmore as he attempted to seize arms and quell unrest. In December 1775, Dunmore moved his forces from Norfolk to fortify Great Bridge and cut off eastern North Carolina from that important port.

According to the legend, Outer Banks resident Sammy Jarvis heard about the news on the mainland and returned home to tell his neighbor Joe Dowdy that if "Dunmore beats our folks at Great Bridge then our goose is cooked and our property is all gone—all the gold and goods saved in our life's work and all our cattle and marsh ponies," according to Creecy's book. The story goes that Betsy Dowdy, part of a family with a long history in Currituck County, overheard Jarvis, left the house and went to the marsh not far away. She called into the darkness for her Banker horse named Black Bess. She mounted Bess and began the ride of many miles to the next nearest North Carolina militia, which was in the town of Hertford in Perquimans County.

She began riding on her horse about midnight, wading and swimming across the cold and shallow Currituck Sound to get to the mainland. She then galloped fifty miles on the tenacious horse to Hertford to notify General William Skinner of the battle brewing in Great Bridge. Skinner heeded the warning and headed north. Dunmore was soundly defeated and eventually left his position as the Virginia governor. Although Skinner arrived too late to make a difference in the battle, his forces ensured the British would not advance into northeastern North Carolina.

Edmund Ruffin, a Virginia politician, planter and writer, described in 1860 how locals corralled wild Banker ponies for domestication. He told of how they could endure hardship and adapt to eating coastal vegetation and drinking brackish water. "I had supposed that the stock, (in the wild state) had ceased to exist there and did not suspect that wild horses, and in much greater number, still were on the narrow sand-reef of North Carolina."[23]

Today, the Banker ponies living on North Carolina's coast number about 220 in total, including herds in Corolla and Shackleford Banks and on Ocracoke Island.

Domestic horses lived on the Outer Banks as well. In the mid-twentieth century, ranchers raised livestock on the Currituck Outer Banks. The U.S. Coast Guard used a mounted patrol of domestic horses on the Corolla beaches during the 1940s. Locals tamed some of the mustangs for rounding up cattle and pulling carts, but as development increased, cattle ranching became untenable. By the 1980s, the wild horses lived in harems of five to

The U.S. Coast Guard once conducted mounted patrols on the Corolla beaches using domestic horses. *Currituck County.*

eight individuals as they do now, surviving on their own, untethered from farm work or fences.

A poster hangs in the wild horse museum and gift shop in Corolla as part of the exhibits describing characteristics of Corolla's wild horses. Corolla horses have shorter backs and smooth muscles, rounded rumps and low-set tails. Two vertebrae fused together help them endure strenuous conditions and traveling long distances. They are smaller than most domestic horses, standing twelve to fourteen hands at the withers, or the top of the shoulders. A hand is four inches. Most weigh between seven hundred and one thousand pounds.

Invited by Outer Banks native Dale Burrus, the Spanish Mustang Registry assessed the physical characteristics of the Corolla horses and recognized them in 1982 as descendants of the Spanish horses.[24]

The late Burrus was an inspector with the registry and was passionate about the preservation of the Banker ponies. His family had tamed some over the years and rode them on Hatteras Island. He convinced skeptical members of the registry to come to Corolla and examine the Corolla herd.

Corolla wild horses standing on a dune. *Drew Wilson.*

The Spanish Mustang Registry inspected the Banker horses, in particular the Corolla strain, and stated that these horses "are as lineally pure to the 16th century Spanish importations as can be found in North America today, and that they compare closely to the selectively bred South American Spanish derivative stock."

Experts with the registry analyzed the physical characteristics of at least twelve Corolla horses and unexpectedly found each one had eight traits of horses brought from Spain; only six are required to become part of the registry. The eight characteristics were:

- Crescent-shaped nostrils
- A round rather than oblong-shaped cannon bone in the lower leg
- A chestnut—the scab-like place on horse legs—that is usually smaller than a dime
- Five lumbar vertebrae rather than six
- A goose-shaped rump and low-docked tail. The backends of domestic horses are more square, and their tails are attached higher
- Ears that point toward each other at the tip
- Little to no feathering or long hair on the legs

The results helped offset claims by locals in Corolla that the herd had come from domestic horses let loose on the Banks to fend for themselves. Burrus maintained that the horses descended from Spanish horses and were often used domestically by locals in the 1800s and 1900s. To them, they did not seem unusual or wild and would be remembered as domestic stock.

Corolla horses typically come in three colors: black; chestnut, which is reddish brown; and bay, which is a brown coat with black tail, mane and lower legs. A gray color once appeared in Corolla horses but has not for a while.[25] The color is a dominant gene, and the hope is it will appear again.

The horses are intelligent and agile, qualities that made them such excellent battle horses so many generations ago. Yet they are friendly toward people, especially once adopted out of the wild, fed and cared for. They can become great riding horses.

Early efforts to identify the Corolla horses as Spanish mustangs were important to gain widespread attention and preserve the herd, but the Equus Survival Trust (EST) disputes the label of Spanish mustangs and instead recognizes them as Banker ponies, a distinct breed. The group placed the Corolla herd on the critical, nearly extinct list since there are fewer than one hundred breeding mares and fewer than seventy-five annual foals.[26] Only about ten Corolla mares give birth to about seven to ten foals a year. EST classifies the Corolla horses as a feral landrace that are free roaming, living in a unique and isolated area and shaped by natural selection over the last five hundred years. The group is an

Two wild horses stand in profile. *Drew Wilson.*

educational nonprofit organization seeking to protect traditional traits, genetic diversity and purity of historic equine breeds.

No known historical records in Spain prove any Spanish mustangs existed there in the sixteenth, seventeenth or eighteenth centuries, according to Victoria Tollman, executive director of the Equus Survival Trust.[27] Horses brought to the Americas from Spain were not always Spanish horses, she said. "Coming from Spain and being Spanish breeds are not one and the same," she said.

Barb or Berber horses existed in North Africa long before Muslims conquered Spain and brought them to that continent. That does not make them Spanish horses, Tollman said. Early on, explorers brought horses of different types from a variety of bloodlines for riding, work and war. The records did not mention breeds back then, she said.

"They certainly did not bring Spanish mustangs," she said. "They did not exist yet."

Ranchers in South America, Mexico and the Caribbean were breeding horses with traits that made them ride well and functional for work. *Spanish mustang* was a term coined in recent decades to name a type of horse developed in the American Southwest. Many wild horses on the Bureau of Land Management lands today are considered Spanish mustangs, Tollman said. "Spain had no mustangs," Tollman said. "That is an American creation."

The Spanish briefly explored the Carolinas before instead focusing on Florida and California. The English were the dominant settlers in North Carolina almost from the beginning. It is highly unlikely the Banker ponies came from a single breed, she said.

"England and Spain were not allies," she said. "Ask yourself, how and why would pure Spanish horses be there and propagating on the Outer Banks?"

The hope is that DNA collection and research will eventually reveal what mix of breeds came to the Americas and which ones were ancestors of today's wild Banker horse herds, Tollman said. Current DNA studies indicate that the Shackleford Banks and the Corolla herds have not mixed with other breeds in the past century. Puckett is working closely with Tollman to get DNA from each horse in hopes that one day it will tell the herd's entire history. Thousands of breeds existing centuries ago do not exist today, Puckett said. She, like Tollman, seeks to recognize the Corolla Banker ponies as their own distinct breed no matter what their ancestry.

"The truth is, we don't actually know what the heritage of the Bankers are," Tollman said.

Chapter 3

LITTLE RED MAN CAN'T BE FENCED IN

With Star gone, his son Midnight became the leading stallion of the Corolla herd. He took on the same mares, including Baygirl, that Star had romanced and protected for more than a decade. Midnight was a small, sturdy black stallion with a big attitude born in 1987. He often challenged other stallions and then strutted around.[28] Midnight ruled around Corolla village until the horses were moved to the upper beaches in 1995. He later developed a respiratory ailment and was taken from the beach to private property on the mainland to live out his days. In 1991, he sired, with the mare Daisy, a precocious colt that was called Little Red Man and would become as well known as his grandfather Star but for different reasons. This was a trying time for the horses and those trying to protect them. Collisions between horses and vehicles took a heavy toll. Volunteers tried marking the mustangs by shooting them with fluorescent paint so that they could be seen at night by drivers. The paint wore off within days. Orange glow-in-the-dark collars attached with hook-and-loop straps were effective but were tough to attach around a wild horse's neck. The horses often managed to scrape them off.[29]

The women working with the fund cut and sewed the collars themselves. They sold T-shirts, cups and bookmarks to raise money. Early fund founder Dru Hodges wrote children's books about them, with proceeds going to the organization. The fund established a promotional campaign where people could sponsor a horse. For $35, the sponsor received a history of the herd, a bumper sticker that said "I Love My Corolla Wild Horse," a family tree and a 5x7 photo of that horse and a one-year subscription to the fund's newsletter.[30] Volunteers put up signs saying "Wild Horse Crossing" and "Wild Horse Sanctuary," but they were stolen at a steady clip. At one point in the early 1990s, it cost $1,200 to replace six of the missing signs. Most of them were paid for by the people putting them up.[31] Some visitors complained about horse poop in their yards or in the driveways of their rental homes. A local realtor who was a horse advocate bought shovels, painted them gold and offered them as a humorous solution for people to scoop up the leavings themselves.[32]

A journal kept by members of the horse fund revealed the daily efforts of protecting horses from the congestion of people and traffic. In April 1993, a call came in that a barking dog had backed a group of horses against a house. Young boys were hitting a colt among the group with sticks while the boys' mother watched. An outspoken volunteer confronted the boys having fun at the horses' expense.

"I lost it," she recorded without putting her name on the entry. "Horses were moved. Kids and mother told off."

A visiting family found a newborn foal underneath the Corolla beach house they were renting. They unsuccessfully tried to put their infant on its back and take photos. It could have been a tragedy, but both foal and child avoided injury. In one account, a volunteer told a man to stay fifty feet away from the horses even though they were grazing in his yard. He told her he would do as he pleased on his property and that she could call the sheriff if she wanted to. That was a common reaction, and it still happens. Horses are known to walk underneath homes set on pilings as someone is grilling or washing a car. It can be hard to avoid them at times. An entry of May 1993 described that horses named Sienna, Trouble, Two Socks, Precious, Butterscotch, Chance and Reno were fighting and whirling in circles in a public area. "Insanity," was the observation. On the same day, members of a harem belonging to the stallion named M&M and another led by Trouble were fighting in the Whalehead Beach neighborhood for over a half hour. Two people caught in the fray barely escaped unharmed. Realtor Kay Cole remembers stopping to show a client a house. While she was parked in the driveway with the windows down, a brazen wild horse stuck its head in her car window where the client sat. It was shocking and a little frightening to them both. After it happened a few more times, Cole kept the windows rolled up when she parked at a property even when it was hot.[33]

The clashes among people, horses and volunteers happened almost daily. Volunteers chased horses from the road and from crowds. Within an hour,

People jog on the beach among the wild horses. *Drew Wilson.*

stallions were fighting again in the road, and people assembled to watch.[34] Stallions fought each other on beach home lots. Herds grazed on recently created rows of lush lawn grasses. They pilfered from trash cans leftovers that are harmful to their digestive systems. Handouts from visitors such as apples and carrots, fine for domestic horses, were hazardous to the wild creatures. Some horses became aggressive and chased tourists into their cottages.

The young horse named Little Red Man seemed to get into the most trouble. He became well known more for his antics than for the bravery and fire displayed by his grandfather Star. One day, he was easily coaxed up to a second-story deck for a taste of pizza. He climbed gingerly up the exterior steps one at a time. As unlikely as it seems that a horse could climb steps, Little Red Man knew how to adapt and overcome most any obstacle to get food.[35] As he neared his prize, he stumbled and fell from the stairs, striking his head on an outdoor faucet below and tearing a bad cut over his eye. The wound healed over time, but he bore the scar for the rest of his life.

About this time in the mid-1990s, Raymond the mule was born to a donkey that had once been part of a petting zoo in Virginia before being sold and brought down to the Outer Banks.[36] The donkey mated with a mare named Gwen and produced Raymond, which would become one of the more well-known characters among the horses. Raymond was full of himself from the start and later tried to be a stallion without being able to produce offspring; mules are sterile. Nevertheless, he would defend his harem of mares against the largest and most aggressive stallions that challenged him. He was smaller, so he would go low in his battles, biting at the legs. That tactic proved effective.

Another stallion named Amadeo was born about this time and would later in life become a personality beloved by the people, including children who knew him. He narrowly avoided a woeful death himself years later. The approximately twenty horses living in the Corolla village needed to be moved. With help from state senator Marc Basnight, Corolla herd advocates lobbied to move the horses to thousands of acres north of Corolla. Federal officials opposed the plan.[37] Another proposal was to contain the herd within a ten-acre tract next to the lighthouse. State officials offered ideas from the town of Banff in Alberta, Canada, whose residents have to live with a wild elk herd of about nine hundred venturing onto their golf courses, school grounds and downtown streets.[38] State leaders spoke with Banff officials after seeing a story about the elk herd there. The town sits within a national park where protection of wild animals takes precedence. But some of the problems are similar to those with the Corolla wild horses. The elk with their massive antlers attacked tourists and residents, charged cars on the highway, munched grass and defecated on golf courses, school grounds and downtown sidewalks. Elks even killed dogs. A semi-truck was totaled after hitting an elk on the highway. One woman heard noises outside her window and looked to find an elk eating flowers from her garden. She had followed the precaution of putting string around her garden with pie pans attached. The idea was the elk would be frightened by the sound of the pans clanging if they crossed over the string. She banged hard on the window, startling the elk to run. As it lifted its head and bolted, its antlers caught the string and the pie pans. The pans banged together behind it in a loud cacophony as it ran down the street. Meanwhile, her flower garden was destroyed. Park officials attempted to change human behavior instead. Among the recommendations was to use locking garbage cans and carry umbrellas for protection, according to a 1993 article in *The Virginian-Pilot*. People were warned not to feed the elk.

"The elk will be elk," said Sean Meggs, front country supervisor for Banff National Park's warden service in the 1993 story. "What we're trying to concentrate on is the people. There's limited things we can do to change the elk behavior. Most of the time it's us that has to change."

Currituck County had no mandate to protect wild animals first, as the Canadians did. County officials could not impose severe restrictions on the people living in Corolla. Horse advocates pushed to move the horses

The massive post and wire fence as it was not long after construction in 1995. *Drew Wilson.*

north. The fund sent letters to members and others who might be interested asking them what to do with the horses. Should they stay put? Should they be removed from the region to a more remote area, or should they be moved to the four-wheel-drive beach north of Corolla? Fund leaders received thousands of responses supporting the move north.[39]

With that support, herd managers decided in 1994 to move the horses out of the village and place them on approximately eleven miles of mostly undeveloped acres north of Corolla, where there were no paved roads. Several wild horses already lived up there among the dunes, marshes and maritime forests. Only a few people had ever seen them.

The idea was not popular with federal officials who led the Currituck National Wildlife Refuge. The refuge was established on more than four thousand acres in 1984. Wild horses were feral and not part of the natural wildlife, officials said. Again, came the mantra—these horses were once domestic.[40] Moving another twenty horses into the area north of Corolla could destroy grasses consumed by wintering waterfowl, they said. Horse managers and county and federal officials worked for years in the 1990s on a compromise plan suitable to all parties.

The Corolla Wild Horse Fund began raising money for a fence and attempted for months to get permits but was repeatedly denied. The U.S. Army Corps of Engineers finally agreed in 1994 following approval by a state environmental agency and issued a permit. Many locals who drove on the beach and the U.S. Fish and Wildlife Service were among those who opposed the fence.[41] The fund built the wooden post and rail fence five feet tall from ocean to sound at a cost of $35,000. The work took months of labor through heavy underbrush, briars and soggy marsh thick with mosquitoes, snakes and biting flies.[42] The fund had to get another permit to extend the fence into the ocean about one hundred yards using large pilings and steel cables. Otherwise, the horses could easily wade or swim around the fence. This section was too involved for volunteers, and a contractor was hired to construct the ocean barrier. Many people doubted the fence would contain them on the north beach. Horses could still swim around the end if the tide was low, they said. Some adventurous horses proved them right.

The Corolla herd of eleven horses was moved north of Corolla on March 24, 1995. A video called *Wild in Corolla*, narrated by the late Charles Kuralt, recorded parts of the move. It was an eventful and emotional day. The horses would be safer out of the busy village, but the area had been their home for centuries. People living in the village would no longer be able to

Riders take to the beach to try to herd wild horses away from the Corolla village. *Drew Wilson.*

see them daily rambling through their yards and over the beach. Despite the danger to the horses and the aggravation they caused, there were some who regretted seeing them go.

Volunteers herded the horses up the beach on foot, in vehicles and on horses. Hodges rode a draft horse that seemed by instinct to know how to direct the wild herd, she recalled. A few people on horseback from a nearby county helped while others walked the neighborhoods rousting the horses from their normal routines. The object was to get them out of the village and onto the beach, where they could more easily be herded northward to a gate in the ocean-to-sound fence. Volunteers struggled to get the last of them to leave Corolla. Butterscotch led three other horses named Trouble, Greco and Condessa into their hangout at Monteray Shores. The horses trotted through the neighborhood and eventually into other housing developments. They disappeared into thick brush at times. They crossed NC 12 over and over. After hours of work, the volunteers finally guided the horses to the beach and herded them north. Cheers went up when the last of them—Butterscotch and her followers—trotted through the gate. An era was over. Still, horses remembered the green grass and other treats. Even after all that lobbying, laboring to build a fence and shepherding them north, some wily mustangs found ways into the village. Butterscotch and several others continually went around the fence and back into Corolla. They were herded up and returned numerous times. Finally, caretakers of the herd realized some wild horses would not stop roaming into Corolla, and eventually they were adopted out to live other places as domesticated horses. Butterscotch was not the last of the horses to seek out the green grasses of rapidly developing Corolla.

The steel cables between pilings on the ocean barrier were susceptible to the salt water and would over time corrode to the breaking point. The intelligent horses, having fended for themselves for centuries, found breaches in the fence and would step through with a little contorting. The ocean fence was expensive and difficult to maintain. In recent years, a storm ravaged the fence, breaking it in places and causing it to sag in others, forcing fund staff and others to find a quick, inexpensive patch until contractors could come in and replace it. They covered gaps with a fence of metal mesh. The fence not only worked well against horses but was also effective with fish. At high tide, hundreds of sea mullet swam into the mesh and were caught as they would have been in a gill net. The tide fell, revealing a flopping catch fit for the best of commercial fishers.[43] Those images made the rounds in social media and news outlets, prompting herd managers to take the fish-catching patch down. A construction crew later replaced the cables and installed turnbuckles, devices that allowed a tightening of the steel lines without having to replace them.

On occasion, horses still wade into the water at low tides and go around the ends of the fences, especially on the sound side. North winds always blow the water southward, drastically lowering the water level in the Currituck Sound. Horses can walk around the end of the fence through the muck left behind. At times, sand gathered like a snowdrift to the top of the fence, where it passed over the dunes. Horses simply walked over it until crews used a backhoe to clear the sand away. People have broken off boards from the rails to place them under their tires when they became stuck in the deep sand at the entrance to the beach where the pavement ends. Horses would climb over the broken section. A cattle grate was placed at the road to prevent the horses from walking over the pavement into the village. The spaced bars across the road let vehicles pass, but horses were leery of stepping over the bars. On rare occasions, sand fills the grate, allowing the horses to pass over it. Volunteers walked the fence regularly searching for breaks or places where horses could cross. It was a miniature version of cowboys riding fence for cattle ranches in the Old West. Workers clear brush growing close to the fence where it passes through a maritime forest.

The fence north of Corolla gets needed repairs. *Meg Puckett.*

The North Carolina Coastal Resources Commission regularly renews a permit for the fence.

Despite the troublesome maintenance, the barrier has done its job for the most part. Only two horses have been killed on NC 12 since the fence went up. A two-year-old stallion named Greco was hit and killed in 1995 in front of Monteray Plaza just four months after the fence was finished.[44] A mare was killed on the busy road in 1999 and left an eight-week-old foal behind. The mare was part of adventurous Little Red Man's herd that kept getting around the barrier. She had followed him to her death, according to Donna Snow, who with her husband, Gene, would direct the Corolla Wild Horse Fund from 2001 to 2006.[45]

Horses have also been struck on the four-wheel-drive side of the fence. The first was a new foal hit and killed in June 1999 by a driver who was going too fast and had been drinking. He was charged and fined $200.[46]

Wild horses also ventured north over the Virginia line into False Cape State Park and the community of Sandbridge in Virginia Beach. Clashes happened there as well. Three stallions traveled into Sandbridge in 1996. One was hit by a car and had to be euthanized. Another, named Midnight Star, was shot through the jaw. He survived the initial wound, but complications made life miserable for him. A veterinarian discovered later that food was getting into his sinus cavity. He was patched up and set loose in the wild on the Outer Banks again. Later, he was bitten by a venomous snake and died.[47] The Snows were often called to corral delinquent horses and take them back to the four-wheel-drive beaches. They came down on their own time and money.

The Snows were part of a group called Tidewater Western Riders that held rodeos to raise money for the children's hospital in Norfolk. They were experts in managing horses and had the equipment to do it. Donna had been dealing with wild horses from North Carolina since the 1970s, when

Horses often gathered around the Whalehead Club in Corolla before the fence was built. *Elaine Goodwin.*

she was a Virginia Beach animal control officer. When called on, the Snows would travel south with portable corrals that could be set up to help guide the horses into the trailers. It was tough work, and the horses didn't always cooperate. The third stallion among those who traveled over the state line was Little Red Man. Trouble always seemed to follow that horse, but he was much loved for his friendliness and brashness. Typically though, he traveled to his old stomping grounds in the village of Corolla.

The naughty stallion and his mares kept finding ways past the south fence to feast on trash scraps and the verdant lawns, especially those growing in the Corolla Light subdivision. Volunteers kept having to round them up and guide them back to the north side of the fence. Little Red Man was born in the village and lived his first few years roaming around Corolla and its delicacies. It was hard for him to give it up. He just kept coming back. And he was smart enough that a fence was not going to stop him. He was so used to having his photo taken, it seemed like he was posing at times in front of the camera. He took over Star's place as one of the most famous of the wild horses. Little Red Man and his mares once invaded a Corolla farm market and ate about $500 worth of fruit and vegetables. He could not be frightened away by flustered market owners. Herd managers paid the vendor for his damages.[48] A bikini-clad woman ready to go to the beach watched helplessly

38

as the bold stallion appeared, stuck his nose into the open back door of her vehicle and grabbed a banana from a grocery bag. Little Red Man ventured into Corolla so often and caused so much trouble that there was nothing to be done but move him elsewhere for his own safety as well that of others. The fence could not prevent his delinquent ventures.

The Snows with other members of the Tidewater Western Riders arrived on June 18, 1999, to corral Little Red Man for the last time. They had rounded up him and his harem about six times in the previous two years. Lloyd Childers, director of the Outer Banks Conservationists,, described Gene and Donna Snow at the time as experts who were as close to horse whisperers as you could get. The Corolla Wild Horse Fund fell under the Outer Banks Conservationists. If anyone could safely remove Little Red Man, it would be the Snows.

The capture turned into an adventure. The horse simply would not cooperate. It was as if he knew that this would be his last escapade on the Corolla Outer Banks. He was found with four other horses, including a three-month-old colt, on a property in the Whalehead subdivision. They grazed on grass near a volleyball court while dozens of people watched. The colt pranced around, putting on a show for the audience.[49] The horses left the grassy area and crossed the dunes onto the beach. Corolla Fire and Rescue used a truck and an all-terrain vehicle to maneuver the horses off the beach. Herd managers decided it was too risky to try to capture them on the beach among one hundred or more tourists. A volunteer managed to corner Little Red Man on a vacant lot and place a harness on him, a move that ended up not being helpful. The other horses were herded a half mile to the yard around the Whalehead Club, a historic winter home and hunting retreat built in the 1920s. The Snows and others arrived to get him into a trailer. They pulled on the rope attached to his halter. Little Red Man dug his hooves into the ground, resisting with all his weight. He frequently reared and fell back or rolled onto his side, his best strategies of resistance. The team managed to get the wild horse to walk backward toward the trailer. After an hour of wrangling, the horse was near the opening. His captors quickly put up a corral to keep him contained. He flopped to the ground, sat on his butt and then suddenly leaped and fell again, striking Gene Snow with his weight and slamming him against the trailer. Amazingly, Snow was all right except for a bent pair of glasses.

They coaxed Little Red Man with domestic horse treats like carrots, foods not typically desirable for wild horses, but he had eaten them before during his ventures into Corolla. They even tried cupcakes with chocolate icing, a

Little Red Man wades into the water at Dews Island. *Donna Snow.*

flavor Little Red Man was known to like. The horse remained seated on his butt as he stretched forth his nose, lips and tongue for a little taste of the chocolate cupcake. They pulled him from the front and pushed him from the rear. Slowly, he raised back onto his feet and walked into the trailer. The other horses were loaded onto other trailers in minutes. They were kept in a corral near the lighthouse temporarily. The tactic of putting a halter on a wild horse was not part of the methods the Snows had developed and caused confusion among everybody there. The Snows said they would not respond to corral wild horses any longer unless they used their tried and tested methods. No more halters on wild horses, they said.

Little Red Man, two or three of his mares and a colt were transported a few weeks later to Dews Island, a four-hundred-acre tract in the Currituck Sound just offshore from the mainland in Jarvisburg. The island and a clubhouse there are used as a waterfowl hunting lodge. It offered the isolation needed to keep Little Red Man out of trouble. He would live on Dews Island until he died in 2008 after siring several foals.[50] As difficult as Little Red Man was, his friendly yet misbehaving reputation won hearts and helped with raising money. A board member of the William H. Donner Foundation read about the horse, prompting the organization to donate $15,000 in 1999 to the fund.[51] Over the next two years, the Donner Foundation donated a total of $75,000. The foundation is a philanthropic organization based in Tarrytown, New York, with causes that include animal welfare. The money allowed the Corolla Wild Horse Fund to split from the Outer Banks Conservationists and incorporate into its own nonprofit, set up an office and hire Gene and Donna Snow as part-time directors. It was a big job that was a burden too heavy for volunteers. The Snows would now be responsible for the horses, spending countless hours checking on frequent calls about sick horses, stray horses and people interfering with horses.

The Snows had to take an annual census into the backroads and count each horse seen. They also chartered flights over land to help spot others that might be in areas inaccessible by vehicle. The counts continue to this day. Horses were not branded or microchipped but instead were identified by color, markings and home territories. Many were given names. Herd managers conducted as many as six aerial counts annually by helicopter. Aerial counts were compared to field notes from ground observations to get the most accurate assessment.

Chapter 4

BIG CROWDS WANT TO SEE

WILD HORSES

T he fence sparked the growth of a new, prosperous enterprise: wild horse tours. People could no longer easily see the horses in the village. They had to get to the northern banks in a four-wheel-drive vehicle and maneuver over the deep sands. It was easier to pay somebody else who knew where to go, how to get there and had a rugged vehicle that could handle the ride. Driving up there takes practice. Hundreds of trucks a day churn in the sand, making it soft and deep. Maneuvering through the tire ruts is a tough job. Dozens of drivers in sedans bog down in the sand each year and need a tow that can cost $300 or more. The beach can be more firm and easier to drive closer to the surf during low tide. The sand is much deeper closer to the dunes and tougher to negotiate. Drivers have to maneuver past sunbathers and watch for playing children.

People with pickup trucks began taking customers to the north beaches to see the horses. Some took it a step further and brought trailers of domestic horses to the beach. They charged for a ride on their mounts up the banks to see the wild horses. That practice was eventually stopped by the county. Jay Bender's operation, Corolla Outback Adventures, began when his parents began taking people on nature tours in the 1960s from Kill Devil Hills to Corolla before the roads were paved beyond Duck. In the course of the trip, they would see wild horses. Bender evolved his business into a horse tour company. Bob's Wild Horse Tours began in 1996, according to the company website. The company is owned and operated by Bob

Three horses relax on the beach. *Corolla Wild Horse Fund.*

White Jr. His father ran the Inn at Corolla Light in the 1990s. Bob White Jr. recalled that one day, some guests asked about how they could see the wild horses. Bob Sr. offered to take them up there in a rusty Suburban he used to ride on the beach. The impromptu trip was a great success. Other guests wanted to go, too. Bob White Sr. accommodated them, and the demand slowly grew. Friends told him it would make a great business. Bob Sr. convinced his son to start a horse tour business, expand it beyond guests at the inn and offer the service to the general public. He called it Bob's Wild Horse Tours. When Bob Jr. began advertising in Outer Banks publications, the enterprise took off, he said.[52] Others followed, offering a similar experience. Customers pay a fee to ride up the beach and into the remote areas behind the dunes. For around sixty dollars a ticket, about a dozen people seated and strapped in the back of an open vehicle rumble for about two hours over the sandy paths through the sparsely populated community.

Tour drivers serve as guides as they talk about the habitat, the history and the horses. Wild-horse excursions draw hundreds of people a day and help drive the county's tourism industry. Year-round residents have complained from the start to the county and the sheriff's office that tour guides and tourists traveling in their own vehicles were speeding over the unpaved roads and gouging big potholes, ramping up more noise, trespassing on

A child follows behind a Corolla wild horse. *Corolla Wild Horse Fund.*

private property and harassing the horses. The horses are like gold for local businesses, beach house rental companies, the county and the state, which use them in advertisements, on their websites and on social media to attract tourists. Many locals are not happy with the tours, but despite the complaints, officials decided it was better to have regulated tours than to have hundreds of people rambling freely over the roads with no real restrictions and no permits required. The Corolla Wild Horse Fund offers training each year to tour companies about how to best treat the horses, keep their distance and be a good neighbor to the year-round residents. There are rare abuses, but for the most part, tour guides follow the rules. At times, a cute new foal will attract several vehicles full of people. It is an unwritten courtesy that the tour truck move on after a few minutes rather than linger in one place observing one set of horses for too long.

The county began requiring permits for tour companies in 2010 with several new rules. Most tour operators supported the changes.[53] At the time, eight companies were operating forty-five vehicles with a total capacity of 324 people. One of the eight was the Corolla Wild Horse Fund, which offered tours for VIPs. The group has since stopped doing tours but maintains its permit. The tours carried people in Hummers with bench seats in an open bed in the back and Jeeps with open sides and soft tops. Some vehicles sported double-decker seating behind the cab.

Other companies offered self-driven all-terrain vehicles that traveled over the dunes to remote areas. Customers could also rent kayaks on a guided tour along the Currituck Sound with a chance to see horses on the shore. In some cases, guides led a line of eight or more in a convoy going up the beach. The vehicles traversed through the communities from dawn to dusk.

Rules for tour companies can be found on the county website and include:

- Tour vehicles are required to display a valid North Carolina license tag.
- Each tour vehicle is required to display the name of the tour company and the yearly county-issued identification.
- Operation of tours west of the dune line in the four-wheel-drive area of the beach is prohibited prior to 8:00 a.m. and after 8:00 p.m.
- The use of amplified sound is prohibited west of the dune line in the four-wheel-drive area of the beach.

- All traffic laws and county ordinances apply to outdoor tour operators, outdoor tour vehicles and outdoor tour drivers.
- Tour vehicles should stay fifty feet from the wild horses.
- Any driving infraction or outdoor tour operator license violation will result in a citation. The actions of tour drivers impact the tour company. Multiple citations will result in suspension of the outdoor tour operator license.

Chapter 5

HOW MANY HORSES ARE TOO MANY?

In December 1996, Lloyd Childers became director of the Outer Banks Conservationists,[54] which was managing the Currituck Beach Lighthouse and also the Corolla Wild Horse Fund. She came with the understanding that she would not have to worry much about the wild horses since they were now all beyond the fence north of Corolla. Her main job was to focus on administration and upkeep of the Currituck Beach Lighthouse and the two keepers' quarters. Thousands of people a year visited and climbed the beacon. She had plenty to do keeping up with that.

Of course, on the first day at her new job, she was helping to herd wayward horses from the village to the north beaches. For the next five years, she worked closely with volunteers such as Dru Hodges, Gene and Donna Snow and Mary and Pat Riley to deal with horse issues. Childers regularly got calls that a group of horses was loose in the village.

Typically, she could call on volunteers, who on foot would guide the horses from the village to the open beach, where they were more easily managed, and then walk them northward, open a gate in the fence and send them back where they belonged for their own safety. In 1999, after years of debate, a group with representatives from Currituck County, the Corolla Wild Horse Fund and the Currituck National Wildlife Refuge, among others, finally agreed on a plan to manage the herd. The committee still meets quarterly and renders decisions that help guide herd managers. The plan was approved in January 2000.[55] For the most part, the document put in writing what the fund had already been doing. The plan included a requirement for annual

A harem of horses grazes near the lighthouse. *Drew Wilson.*

herd counts and directions on the extent of human intervention, how to control the numbers and when horses would have to be removed from the beach. The most divisive part stipulated that the herd be maintained at sixty horses. Refuge officials insisted that any more than that would damage the habitat. Horses had grazed at least 120 acres of prime waterfowl habitat to the point it could not recover if the foraging continued.[56] A large tract of

A foal kicks up its heels near its mother. *Meg Puckett.*

ponds, wetlands and prime feeding area for ducks was fenced off to keep deer, feral pigs and the horses away.

Despite the plan limits on population, the herd numbers have remained around 100 animals for several years with the unofficial consent from federal authorities. In 2018, after many years of lobbying by herd managers, wildlife officials agreed to let the population grow to a range of 120 to 130 individuals.[57] The management plan signed nearly two decades earlier no longer mandated a maximum number of 60. The change was monumental to the herd. The genetic stability of the horses would be much more assured. Expanding herd numbers is a major step to improving the overall health of the herd, including the genetic pool and its sustainability, according to fund officials. Herd managers reduced the contraceptive program, and mares gave birth to at least 9 foals in 2021, the most in many years. To reduce herd numbers, herd managers injected selected mares with the contraceptive called PZP. By the fall of 2022, 7 foals had been born; 5 survived. Federal wildlife officials agreed that years of studies and observation indicated the horses were not damaging the habitat as much as previously thought. A blend of effective negotiation and better relations between fund officials and federal authorities helped.

Former fund director Karen McCalpin maintains it is still crucial to get a law passed in the U.S. Congress setting the limits of the horse herd at 130 individuals. She fought for about a decade to get a law passed calling for the herd to expand. New federal administrators could later change the herd plan again to require a lower number.[58] Herd managers contend they do not want the herd to be too large and damage the habitat any more than federal rangers do.

Over time, it became obvious that feral pigs were the most destructive animal in the environment. They reproduce quickly and eat most anything. They use their snouts and tusks to gouge large muddy holes, tearing up prime wildlife habitat and uprooting trees that produce acorns and cover. As of 2021, feral pigs were in decline. The habitat was the best it had been in a long time, according to Mike Hoff, manager of the Currituck National Wildlife Refuge. An influx of coyotes preyed on the piglets and drastically reduced their numbers. State and federal efforts had already tried a variety of strategies, including trapping, hunting and even shooting the pigs from helicopters. As the feral pigs declined, so did their predator, the coyotes. It was a case where one pest helped control another pest.[59]

Chapter 6

A KILLER SHOOTS THEM DOWN

I n one of the most tragic events of the wild herd, four horses and a mule were found shot to death in November 2001. Corpses of a horse and a mule were discovered at the intersection of Shark Lane and Salmon Road, two of the crisscrossing sand roads in Carova Beach about two miles south of the Virginia line. Three other decomposing horses were found in the following days. A stallion dead from a gunshot wound turned up on the nearby beach.[60] Within a day or two, four horses and a mule had been shot and another horse intentionally struck by a vehicle.

It was a shock to the community, who quickly called on the Currituck Sheriff's Office to investigate the deaths as if they were homicides. Locals reported hearing gunshots two days before the first horse was found. Detectives examined the carcasses for clues. They found bullet holes in the bodies but, despite using metal detectors, could not find any bullet casings. No witnesses came forth despite numerous interviews of people living nearby. Investigators had no suspects, no motive and no good leads. It was not certain whether the shots were from close range or from a distance. The horses were buried without autopsies because of the decomposition and the difficulty of hauling corpses several miles down the beach. The investigation led to interviews with people throughout the region without any good breaks, and the case was never solved. It probably never will be, a deputy who helped investigate the case said in a 2021 interview.

The sheriff would not release reports even twenty years later, calling it an open investigation.

Not many people lived in Carova Beach year-round. The community of a couple hundred permanent residents ballooned to several thousand on any given day during the summer season. Visitors increase in November leading up to Thanksgiving. Investigators had no way of knowing if the shootings were done by a local resident or someone staying here for a few days. It was likely someone drove by and shot them from a vehicle and then ran over another one. Was the killer drunk and did it on a whim, or was it premeditated for some reason? The shootings outraged avid wild horse advocates across the nation. As if there weren't enough threats to the herd, here was another one that was unprecedented. The mustangs had been moved from the dangerous traffic and congestion in Corolla, and now it was the very isolation of the northern four-wheel-drive beach that could hide anyone who would shoot them. Questions and fears arose over whether this would keep happening. Many believed that someone who killed innocent horses could also kill people. Locals and visitors alike were alarmed. The horse fund offered a $5,200 reward for information that was augmented by others for a total of $13,360.[61] The offer still stands twenty years later, according to herd manager Meg Puckett.

In the end, these were horses, not people, and law enforcement could not expend but so much time on the case. There were typically only one or two deputies assigned to patrol the Currituck Outer Banks. The most serious charge might have been felony animal cruelty with a fine and up to fifteen months in prison.[62] When the initial investigation of the scene was over, longtime local resident and landowner Ernie Bowden buried the horses in the sand in the area where they lived.

Through all the bloodshed, one weak little four-month-old colt that was part of that tragic harem survived. He stood out from the others. Monto'ac was the first painted horse born among the wild herd in at least twenty-five years. The colt was smaller than normal and had one blue eye and one brown eye. He was well known to herd managers.[63] Those characteristics alone would draw attention, but Monto'ac was orphaned shortly after his birth and barely escaped death at least twice. His name is an Algonquian word for supernatural being, and in this case it might be true. Authorities think the colt's mother was among those shot intentionally or hit and killed by a vehicle. Horse herd managers hoped the little colt could remain with the wild herd and find a new family. For a while, he hung out with another small, orphaned horse named Elmer. One day, a real estate agent taking

A horse strolls on the boardwalk within the Currituck Banks Estuarine Research Reserve. *Drew Wilson.*

photographs of vacant lots found Monto'ac lying in the grass barely alive. It was believed he had been attacked by a stallion. He did survive the encounter, his second brush with death. This time, he was removed from the wild herd. The painted colt was taken to recuperate at the Snows' farm in Virginia Beach and was doing well until he was attacked by a pack of wild dogs. He survived and healed over time. Monto'ac has since lived a long and peaceful life at the Snows' farm and was doing well as of 2022.[64] Time passed without more intentional shootings in Carova Beach, to the relief of everyone.

Another horse was shot in 2004 that was likely an accident where a hunter within the Currituck Banks Reserve mistook a wild mare for a feral pig, according to the investigating officer and records of the Currituck County Sheriff's Office. The horse was standing behind a large fallen tree in dim light under the forest canopy. The state issued permits for hunters to kill feral pigs within its boundaries. The pigs proliferated quickly and tore up the habitat badly. Hunting was a strategy to keep them in check. But horses also occasionally roam in there. The thick canopy darkens the woods and makes it hard to see, especially early and late in the day. A pregnant mare was shot and killed around Christmas 2005. That case was never solved but was also believed to be a hunting accident, according to a deputy who investigated. A hunter found a stallion shot to death in November 2007 in a marshy area within the Currituck Banks Reserve in another unsolved incident.

Chapter 7

ANOTHER FENCE AND MORE LAWS

PROTECT THE HERD

T he fence near Corolla was for the most part effective in keeping the horses out of the village. Eleven miles north at the Virginia state line, horses wandered into False Cape State Park, Back Bay National Wildlife Refuge and the Virginia Beach neighborhood of Sandbridge. The Corolla fence had worked well enough that herd managers were convinced a sound-to-sea barrier on the state line would, too. In January 2003, horse fund members and volunteers from both sides of the line constructed a fence about a mile long just north of the state line within False Cape State Park.[65] A short fence with a gate had been built in the 1970s over the beach and dunes to keep traffic from traveling through the park and the refuge. It did not reach across the entire strand, but it was enough to keep people from driving up the beaches into the parks and disturbing the beach habitat.

State park officials allowed about one hundred residents of the Currituck north banks who frequently traveled the beach to have keys to the gate. It was unpopular, and locals called it the "iron curtain."[66] Access through the gate could not be sold or passed on to heirs. Eventually, the privilege of driving north to Virginia Beach over the beach through the parks will go away. Only a handful of people can still pass through now. Fund officials and volunteers connected the new fence to the existing barrier, and for the most part, it kept horses from venturing into Virginia.

Neither fence stopped all bad interactions between people and horses as crowds to the four-wheel-drive beach north of Corolla grew. A cadre of horse advocates who live in the four-wheel-drive area kept watch and still

Two horses walk along a sandy road in Carova Beach. *Meg Puckett.*

do. These volunteers report to fund officials when they see distressed horses or tour guides not following the rules, among other violations. Social media has intensified the discovery and public display of encroachments. Despite all the prevention efforts, people still get too close too often. On a summer day, a dog without a leash barked and snarled at a group of wild horses on the beach. It was recorded and posted on social media, where hundreds blasted the dog owners as irresponsible and fretted over the well-being of the horses. The outcry was not necessary. The wild horses that have fought for their survival for hundreds of years took care of things. One horse turned and kicked the dog, sending him yelping. At the same time, another charged him, chasing the dog from what he thought was going to be fun.

The Snows resigned in 2006, citing differences with the fund board on how to manage the herd and to continue working their farm in Virginia Beach, where they keep about a dozen domesticated Corolla wild horses.[67] The Snows also run a nonprofit called Virginia Wild Horse Rescue with responsibilities of capturing and returning wayward horses that roam into False Cape State Park and Virginia Beach. The influx of people to the northern Currituck banks and all the interaction between them called for full-time management of the fund.

After the Snows resigned, the fund hired Karen McCalpin as full-time director and Steve Rogers as herd manager, thanks to an $85,000 loan from Currituck County.[68] The fund also bought its first four-wheel-drive vehicle to better reach the boonies of the banks. The county loan was later forgiven. McCalpin, of Pennsylvania, was experienced in nonprofit management and had owned and trained horses for more than four decades.

Herd managers hired aspired to the unique job of working with wild horses, but until Puckett, they stayed a relatively short while and moved on. The first new herd manager, Steve Rogers, had worked with horses since he was fourteen. He was trained in horse care and breeding, gaining experience working on a Texas ranch and as a stable manager in Louisburg, North Carolina.[69] Three years later, he left, and Wesley Stallings replaced him. Stallings graduated from North Carolina State University with a degree in agricultural business. He had worked for more than twenty years in the equine and livestock industry and had competed in rodeos and horse shows across the country.[70] In 2014, Christina Reynolds, of central North Carolina, was hired to replace Stallings. She had trained horses since her childhood. She stayed almost two years.[71] McCalpin and herd managers had the hard job of trying to maintain the herd number at 60 horses to comply with the management plan signed in 2000. At the same time, a larger herd was important for good genetic quality and health of the herd. It was a tough

Horses stand on the beach near a crowd of people. *Drew Wilson.*

Above: Karen McCalpin was the first full-time director of the Corolla Wild Horse Fund. *Karen McCalpin.*

Left: A mother and her foal graze on the beach. *Meg Puckett.*

balance. McCalpin would be a strong advocate of increasing the size of the herd. In 2006, 25 new foals were born, and the herd numbers climbed to about 120 horses, possibly the most in decades.[72]

That raised the hackles of federal officials again, who continued to warn that too many horses were bad for the habitat. They were reminding the herd managers that they had been easy on the sixty-horse mandate called for the in the management plan, but this surge was too much. They tested their theory by fencing off areas within the Currituck National Wildlife Refuge to exclude horses, feral hogs and deer. They believed that would show the waterfowl feeding areas would improve if left alone by the unwanted grazers. One of the concerns about fencing is that the metal can rust and detach from posts, becoming a choking or entanglement hazard for horses. Barbed wire can badly cut an animal trying to fight its way over it. Even so, herd managers were forced to reduce the horse population to comply with the demands of federal wildlife officials under the management plan. An aggressive program to lessen the population was started. After the banner year of births in 2006, roughly twenty horses were adopted out, and eight others died of natural causes or were transferred from the Currituck Outer Banks for other reasons. Between 2006 and 2016, the fund adopted out more than fifty horses.[73] In the meantime, McCalpin gathered scientific data in hopes of getting the management plan population mandate increased to better reflect the endangered status of the horses, she said.

In February 2007, McCalpin hosted representatives from the Horse of the Americas (HOA) and the Livestock Conservancy as part of an effort to confirm the herd descended from colonial Spanish mustangs. That would bring about even more widespread recognition of the herd, justify enlarging its size and protect their endangered breed status. The HOA, an international nonprofit organization, keeps a registry of the horses related to the original Native American horses and the colonial Spanish mustang, among others. The Livestock Conservancy identifies, tracks and works to protect endangered livestock and poultry breeds from extinction. The equine experts reported that these hardy horses showed characteristics of colonial Spanish mustangs.[74] They measured wild horses that had been adopted and domesticated from skull to tail. They investigated a pile of horse bones in Corolla for clues. They noted how they walked, the shape of their hips and even how they stored fat. The Corolla herd has only twenty-nine alleles, a genetic indicator showing they lack diversity. It is among the lowest number of any horse population, according to the HOA report. The genetic indicators showed that this herd could not have been diluted with domestic breeds over the years, according to the report.

There is less genetic diversity among the Corolla group than any other group of horses, it said. They are a breed unto themselves that resembles the old Iberian horses. Like the Spanish Mustang Registry did some quarter century earlier, Horse of the Americas concluded the old herd descended from Spanish horses. The horses were registered as colonial Spanish mustangs in 2007 by the Horse of the Americas.

Herd handlers turned to a more intensive approach to reducing the population. In 2007, herd manager Steve Rogers began injecting aged, sickly or very young mares with porcine zona pellucida or PZP, a birth control chemical that must be given annually. The goal was to trim the herd. He recorded each dose administered.[75] Wild horses were not going to sit still for a hand-delivered shot in the backside. Instead, Rogers, loaded a rifle with a dart, walked to within three hundred yards of chosen mares and shot them in the rump with a dart from a CO_2 rifle. The dart would pop out right away. Mares would jolt a little after the shot and then keep on grazing. PZP stimulates the mare's immune system to produce antibodies that block sperm receptors. Each dose of the contraceptive cost twenty-one dollars. The drug had a proven track record after being successfully used on more than fifty different mammal species. Assateague Island National Seashore managers had successfully injected horses in an effort that began with trials in 1998.[76]

Some groups contend that PZP has unwanted side effects, but the evidence for safe use is strong, according to Corolla herd managers. The contraceptive program in Corolla was conducted under guidelines from the Humane Society of the United States and the Science and Conservation Center in Billings, Montana. The staff is trained in how to safely deliver PZP. Herd managers still administer PZP by CO_2 pistol or rifle or with blowguns. The plan worked very well.

A group of horses trots down the beach. *Drew Wilson.*

By 2008, herd numbers had dropped to about 90, which was much closer to the 60 stipulated by the management plan. McCalpin remained concerned that too few horses would mean a low genetic diversity, a condition that could lead to health issues and birth defects in the herd. Research by Dr. Gus Cothran, a geneticist with Texas A&M University, showed as much.[77] DNA testing of 17 horses in 1993 indicated a small gene pool in the Corolla herd, which could lead to a higher incidence of disease and birth defects, according to a report at the time by Cothran.[78] Corolla horses are genetically similar to the Shackleford horses and closely related to the original horses of the Iberian Peninsula. The study did not prove the horses were Spanish mustangs but did indicate they had genes unique to the Outer Banks herd.[79] Cothran concluded again in 2008 that the Corolla herd lacked genetic diversity and recommended the herd expand to at least 120 and preferably 150. Cothran's conclusions were another part of the argument for a change in the law to expand the herd up to 130 individuals.

Deadly interactions further reduced the herd. A stallion was struck in March 2009 on the beach in Carova and was found later with a broken leg. He had to be euthanized. Investigators never found out who hit the horse.

In May, the well-known chestnut stallion called Spec was found near the same location with a badly broken leg and also had to be euthanized. In this case, the driver was identified and charged.[80] The community was outraged at the deaths. Whoever hit them left without reporting the incident. Both horses were hit low on their legs, indicating they were likely struck by an all-terrain vehicle, beach Jeep or dune buggy.

"Whoever did this has no conscience," McCalpin said.[81]

In October, a deputy on patrol late at night along the northern beaches accidentally collided with a horse.[82] Two stallions were chasing each other and had not seen the vehicle. One stallion rammed into the deputy's patrol truck, reminiscent of how Star died. The horse was injured so badly, with broken legs and other injuries, that it had to be put down. Other interactions had the potential for injuries to both humans and horses. So far, no person has been killed or severely injured by a wild horse, but that might be more from luck rather than caution. Two young boys walked up to a black stallion watching over his harem of Corolla wild horses and began patting him on the rear. The boys' mother sat on a sand dune nearby, apparently unconcerned. A volunteer with the wild horse sanctuary patrol quickly approached and asked the boys to slowly back away. The horse could have easily kicked them and killed them. Herd managers and volunteers ask themselves what people are thinking, especially parents, when they allow something like that.

To stem dangerous encounters, Currituck County amended an ordinance to make it illegal to intentionally come within fifty feet of a wild horse. The law previously banned luring a horse to within fifty feet. Violations bring a $500 fine.[83]

A mother and father tried to put their child on the back of a wild horse and take a photograph, though it never worked out; the horse would not allow it. A woman somehow inserted herself into the midst of a few horses and walked with them along the beach. She emerged from this dangerous encounter without harm. A group from a rental cottage left the porch with cameras to get close-ups of wild horses, prompting a stallion to charge from a nearby sand dune. The family rushed back, barely making it to the safety of the porch. Conflicts with people either ignorant of the rules or ignoring them continued. In the spring of 2012, a stallion named Two Socks, perhaps the grandson of Star, was hit and killed by a passing vehicle late in the evening. He was standing on the shoreline when he was struck.[84] Two Socks was eight to ten years old, and his grandsire had lived with the herd in Corolla before the fence went up. Fund officials and many in the beach community were heartbroken over his death.

A young wild horse named Tanner was found very sick, barely able to stand and with his ribs showing. He had classic symptoms of malnutrition, an uncommon malady for a young foal with a healthy, attentive mother. A vet tried to save him by inserting a tube through his nose to his stomach to administer water and a lubricant, a common treatment for colic. It was no use. He died a few days later. The foal suffered miserably for days before dying. A necropsy showed the foal's intestines were impacted and infected, almost certainly the result of its eating something besides mother's milk and natural foods. People had been seen feeding the foal and its parents watermelon rinds, an obvious violation of the Currituck County ordinance and of the warnings given by herd managers. Food that domestic horses eat without problems can sicken or kill wild horses.

The bad interactions became so frequent that volunteers reporting what they saw was not enough. McCalpin hired five officers to patrol the beaches. Four of the officers were Currituck County sheriff's deputies working during off-duty hours.[85] In 2009, Currituck County banned owning or riding domestic horses in the four-wheel-drive area. It was another effort to reduce wild horse deaths.[86]

Even vaccinated domestic horses can carry diseases and parasites that can be fatal to wild horses. Corolla mustangs are not vaccinated. Any exposure could quickly spread through the herd. Among the worst natural ailments

Left: The wild horse named Two Socks stands near the surf. *Karen McCalpin.*

Below: The car that struck Two Socks was badly damaged. *Karen McCalpin.*

is a disease called the strangles caused by a bacteria found among domestic horses. The strangles cause abscesses that can form in the neck and mouth area and rupture. Lymph nodes swell and block the respiratory tract, making breathing difficult. Horses lose their appetites. A case broke out in eastern North Carolina in recent years not far from the Corolla beaches. Puckett and others constantly changed their clothes after working with their personal domestic horses. They did not want the disease spreading into the wild herd.[87] Fortunately, none of the wild horses caught the malady.

Watermelon is not good for wild horses. People should not feed them. *Meg Puckett.*

Equine influenza or horse flu can also spread rapidly through a herd. Nasal discharge, a cough and weakness are among the symptoms. Some horses show no signs of the illness yet can be carriers. Wild stallions tend to challenge unknown horses without worrying about whether they are domestic or not. People might even be riding on them. A wild stallion charged a group riding horses along the beach. One horse reared, throwing its rider, and then galloped through a crowd of tourists.[88] Domestic horses could also introduce invasive plants to the Currituck National Wildlife Refuge through their dung. An invasive plant can overtake vital native vegetation important to waterfowl.

Not everyone agreed with the ban of domestic horses. Longtime resident Ernie Bowden made the point that if wild horses were so susceptible to problems from domestic livestock, they should have died long ago. In the mid-1900s, Bowden and his neighbors owned farms on the northern banks raising horses, sheep, goats, hogs, cattle, chickens and even buffalo. The U.S. Coast Guard used mules and horses for beach patrol and to haul rescue boats and equipment.

In 2010, McCalpin continued raising the profile of the wild horses and their importance as a breed. She spoke with Currituck County teachers who said they were seeking history subjects that would interest boys and girls alike for state-mandated writing tests. She suggested learning about the heritage of the wild horses and then writing letters to elected officials to get the Corolla mustangs designated as the state horse. It had been on her mind for a while. On a selected school day, McCalpin took a horse to Shawboro

Corolla wild horses graze near the Currituck Beach Lighthouse. *Drew Wilson.*

Longtime Currituck Beach resident Ernie Bowden stands next to one of his domestic horses. Bowden raised cattle in the Carova Beach area. *Drew Wilson.*

A foal rests in the shade. *Drew Wilson.*

A man runs next to wild horses many years ago. People are not supposed to get within fifty feet of the wild horses. *Drew Wilson.*

Stallions fight each other for control of a harem of mares. *Erin Millar.*

Egrets perch on the backs of wild horses to eat insects. *Corolla Wild Horse Fund.*

Horses stand on the beach near an old lifesaving station converted to a real estate office. *Currituck County.*

Stallions spar over dominance. *Currituck County.*

A wild horse wades in a canal. *Currituck County.*

Horses graze near a large beach house. *Currituck County.*

Horses stroll on the beach. *Currituck County.*

Horses graze on the dune. *Currituck County.*

Horses walk along one of the many sandy backroads in the four-wheel-drive area north of Corolla. *Currituck County.*

Horses walk along the beach. *Currituck County.*

A lone horse stands near the dunes. *Currituck County.*

A horse walks near the surf in the bright sunshine. *Erin Millar.*

A harem of wild horses hangs out on the beach. *Erin Millar.*

Horses stand among the sand fences used to help hold the dunes in place. *Erin Millar.*

A horse rolls in the sand. *Erin Millar.*

Two horses splash in the surf. *Erin Millar.*

Wild horses relax during the outgoing tide. *Erin Millar.*

The sun and sand feel good to this harem of wild horses. *Erin Millar.*

Horses run in the surf. *Erin Millar.*

A horse trots along the surf. *Erin Millar.*

Horses on the beach with sand fences in the background. *Erin Millar.*

Horses hanging out at the beach. They often come to the ocean to get away from black biting flies more prevalent in the thickets behind the dunes. *Erin Millar.*

Horses staying near the beach where they are often seen by crowds of people. *Erin Millar.*

Horses relaxing in the low tide. *Erin Millar.*

A lone horse surveys its surroundings. *Erin Millar.*

A pair of wild horses runs along the beach. *Drew Wilson.*

Elementary School, where the mascot name is fittingly the mustangs.[89] Students from kindergarten through the fifth grade were bused in from other elementary schools as well. McCalpin showed the features of the wild horse outside while others gave a Power Point presentation indoors on their history and habitat. The schools held a contest for the best letter written to elected officials about the horses. The focus was to convince legislators to designate the mustangs the state horse. The winner earned a savings bond and a trip to see the horses in their beach environment. Second- and third-place prizes were also awarded. The campaign spread as hundreds of letters from schoolchildren were sent to Bill Owens, a state representative at the time. The General Assembly passed the bill, and Governor Beverly Perdue signed it into law in 2010. The recognition added another level of importance to the herd and bolstered odds for their further protection.

Chapter 8

MCCALPIN GOES TO WASHINGTON

One of Karen McCalpin's most important goals was to get a law in place that would override the management plan that called for 60 horses and allow expansion of the herd. U.S. representative Walter Jones, representing eastern North Carolina, sponsored bills year after year from 2008 to 2017 that specified the herd would be managed at between 120 and 130 individuals and never fall below 110.[90] Jones had sponsored similar legislation that became law in the 1990s protecting the Shackleford Banks horses. The Corolla bill repeatedly passed the House but did not get through the Senate, according to congressional records. In the last attempt, it passed both houses, but a bipartisan committee that was to review it before sending it to the president never met.[91]

Federal wildlife officials opposed the legislation, always with concerns that more wild horses would damage refuge habitat. They wanted the herd to remain at the limit of sixty stipulated in the management plan.

"Native species that depend upon this coastal barrier island ecosystem include waterfowl, wading birds, shore birds, raptors, mammals, reptiles, amphibians and a variety of plants," said Greg Siekaniec, acting deputy director of the U.S. Fish and Wildlife Service.[92] "The refuge provides habitat for endangered species such as piping plover and sea turtles.

Siekaniec continued, "The Service views wild horses as feral domestic animals. On the refuge, horses compete with native wildlife species for resources and often negatively impact habitat. For example, horses trample and consume plants, removing food and shelter for native species. Horses are also known to facilitate the introduction of invasive weeds."

Wild horses graze in a meadow. *Meg Puckett.*

In 2012, Ducks Unlimited sent a letter to Senator James Inhofe to express objections to a larger herd.[93] They felt the waterfowl habitat was already under duress. Wild horse grazing would only destroy more of a scarce resource.

McCalpin responded with several counterpoints that still apply.[94] She wrote that annual aerial counts show that at least three-quarters of the herd and possibly more live on privately owned land, not the refuge. A herd count in 2012 yielded 121 horses, one of the highest counts ever. Of those, 8 horses were seen scattered on refuge land during the count, evidence of their minimal impact, she wrote. McCalpin traveled to Washington on two occasions to lobby for the bill's passage. On the last trip, she went from one senator's office to another all day. She walked so much the sole of one of her shoes became loose and flapped as with each step.[95] Exhausted and exasperated, she and her husband ate dinner at a nice restaurant later that evening. She did not have time to buy new shoes, so she used chewing gum to hold the sole in place while at the restaurant.

McCalpin worked for years to build a case for passage of the law, including helping to get the mustangs designated as the state horse, by further establishing their heritage through Horse of the Americas and by promoting them with pamphlets and billboards. The failure of that bill to pass over all those years was one of the biggest disappointments of her life, McCalpin said. She felt strongly the law was needed for a larger and genetically healthier herd. McCalpin retired after eleven years in Corolla and returned to her home state of Pennsylvania. She remains involved in protecting wild horses across the country as a member of the Cloud Foundation, a national organization based in Colorado. She is an outspoken critic of the slaughter of wild and domestic horses.

Another director was hired weeks later after a national search only to have her leave following a short stint. It is not clear why. To replace her, Jo Langone was hired as the fund's chief operating officer. She had worked with the fund in administrative positions since 2014. Before coming to Corolla, she worked in management and sales and marketing in the hospitality industry. Herd manager Meg Puckett of Kill Devil Hills was hired by McCalpin in 2016 after working in public relations and education with the Norfolk Zoo in Virginia and the Museum of the Albemarle in Elizabeth City, North Carolina. She had wanted this job since she was a child and gazed at the poster of Star on her wall.[96]

Chapter 9

BRIARS TASTE GOOD

The herd continues to thrive despite the horrific ways they could die either naturally or through clashes with people. The habitat furnished enough food and cover, and the horses reproduced well. Between the fences, Corolla's wild horses live in an area eleven miles long and about a mile wide. The range includes about twelve thousand acres of five primary coastal habitats: brackish marsh, maritime forests, grassy meadows, shrub thickets and beaches and dunes.[97] Some of the acres are fenced off within the Currituck National Wildlife Refuge. Part of the territory includes dozens of marshy islands, creeks and ponds. Occasionally, the horses spend time on one of the islands and may not be seen for a while.

The horses have acclimated to the habitat and thrive without human help. The constant winds carrying salt and sand don't bother them. They easily find refuge among the thickets or under the canopy of the live oaks. Autopsies of wild horses that died showed they rarely have parasites because of their good, natural diet.[98] The different types of vegetation transition consistently east to west from the beach to shrubs, to meadows, to forests and finally to marshes along the sound. The pattern is largely the same throughout the northern Outer Banks, allowing the twenty or so harems of horses to separate into territories. Each band averaging four or five horses has access to the same food and cover.

Their territories are only general boundaries, and occasionally, stallions fight over who this space belongs to. Within the area where the horses roam, the Currituck National Wildlife Refuge encompasses roughly 4,570 acres in

Left: An aerial view of the wild environment demonstrates the variety of habitat. *Meg Puckett.*

Below: Horses walk along the thick brush. *Drew Wilson.*

the north beach area and another 3,931 acres in easements.[99] The nearby Currituck Banks Estuarine Reserve contains roughly 1,000 acres. Developers platted 3,400 lots in the 1960s and 1970s on the remaining privately owned land.[100] The communities were planned with the idea that people would travel southward from Virginia Beach on paved roads. Formation of False Cape State Park and Back Bay National Wildlife Refuge eliminated the chance of a highway from Virginia Beach. As of 2021, 840 homes dot the area in small communities behind the dunes, nearly double what it was two decades ago.[101] The large, multistory homes line much of the oceanfront. Smaller, more modest homes typically populate lots along back roads and canals on the sound side.

Right: Horses graze near the roadside thickets. *Meg Puckett.*

Below: A foal plays next its mother close to a large home. *Meg Puckett.*

The Corolla Wild Horse Fund maintains an account set aside for buying land in the north beaches. So far, the group has purchased five lots totaling about five acres. Jay Bender, owner of Outback Adventure Tours, donated more than sixty acres as part of a conservation easement. A part of that area has a wide-open meadow with few trees or roads, a haven for grazing and finding fresh water collected in depressions.[102] The horses also enjoy lawns, artificially planted to beautify rental homes. The horses have evolved over the centuries to survive on the native plants such as coarse salt grass, sea oats, panic grass, beach grass and cordgrass. They munch on persimmons, greenbrier, wax myrtle, cattails and acorns fallen to the ground from live oaks—all unexpected fare for a horse. Milfoil is an invasive plant growing

Horses cool off in one of the man-made canals in Carova Beach. *Meg Puckett.*

in the sound that can clog the waterway and block sunlight to the bottom. Native aquatic plants can struggle to survive in its presence. The horses wade in the sound and creeks, poke their noses into the water and grab mouthfuls of milfoil to chew, helping to clear the waterway and admit more sunlight to native vegetation.[103]

Plants like greenbrier and wax myrtle that seem like they might be distasteful grow prodigiously in the humid Outer Banks environment. Wax myrtles with small green leaves grow in thickets along the sandy roads the horses use as pathways. Piles of droppings from horses dot the roadways, evidence of their habit of grazing the brush along the shoulder. Greenbrier keeps its leaves until late winter and provides cold-weather food for wildlife such as deer, rabbits and wild horses. It grows as a thorny vine climbing up other plants. Landscapers consider it a pest, but it is important in a coastal habitat. Horses also graze in the cold months on such plants as silver-leaf croton and salt meadow hay, known as cordgrass. Many coastal grasses turn brown during the winter but still contain nutrients. Croton plants that grow in clusters with fuzzy leaves are resistant to salt air, grow on the dunes and are hardy, much like the horses. The plants can survive being buried in sand for long periods. Salt meadow cordgrass, or salt meadow hay, looks like a wavy green meadow and grows in the lowlands west of the dunes. The stems are blown by the wind, giving it a whorled appearance like thick, uncombed hair.

Sugar-filled winter lawn grasses might stay green but are sort of like fast food for horses—tasty and convenient but not as good for them.[104] As the grasses turn green and the weather warms in the spring, the horses tend to move eastward, closer to the beach. Dune grasses return for summertime feasts. Horses frequently munch on the manicured lawns and stand under the cover of the beach homes. Renters thrill at taking photos and videos from their decks as horses lounge below. New foals kick up their spindly legs and suddenly burst into short runs around their mothers in front of excited beach house guests. The horses have plenty of water sources. They drink from the brackish sound, marsh ponds and the man-made canals. They wade into the fresh water to drink, cool off and escape biting flies. Developers dug miles of canals decades ago to create more waterfront parcels.

The canals can be deadly on occasion. A few years ago, a group of horses casually crossed a canal, as they often do. One of the mares stepped in a hole and went under. She apparently panicked and drowned in a few minutes, falling to the hazards of her habitat. In 2021, a foal named Beatrice nearly

A horse walks near a thicket that provides food and cover. *Currituck County*.

drowned in a canal until a group of fishermen saw her and pulled her to safety.[105] Large, deep potholes the size of small ponds form on the sandy roads. Traffic from off-road vehicles is surprisingly busy, ever wearing on the unpaved roads. The water in the potholes is deep enough to rise to the hood of a truck. The horses generally know better than to drink from the water possibly polluted with gas or oil.

A few acres of marshy bogs exist in the middle of neighborhoods. Horses know to go into these handy wetlands for a consistent source of food, and they can blend unseen among the reeds growing in them. Storms are a common part of life on the Outer Banks. The wild horses retreat to the thick maritime forests on higher ground, an area rarely seen by visitors. They can sense the drop in pressure when a tropical storm approaches. The canopy works like an umbrella. They stand amid the cover on the west side of the banks on higher ground where live oaks, swamp black gum, red maple, cypress and pines grow. Live oak limbs with their rough bark angle downward close to the ground, creating a perfect back-scratching post for horses.

Extra protection and food come from a thick understory of wax myrtle, swamp red bay, holly and dogwood. Horses travel unseen through narrow paths in the thickets, much like deer. Wild horses grow a thicker coat in cold weather, and the fur fluffs up to create insulation. The coat of a wild horse in the winter can look almost bear-like.

A foal and its mother are silhouetted on a dune. *Corolla Wild Horse Fund.*

Wild horses gather under the porch of a beach home. *Drew Wilson.*

In the summer, they gather at the beach to get away from biting flies and cool off. Help comes from cattle egrets, lanky white birds that hang around to eat the bugs. Like best buddies, the birds stand on the horses' backs to gobble flies.

Wild horses trim their own hooves by constant travel looking for food and water on the Outer Banks. The sand and other soils naturally keep their hooves worn down. Through natural selection, horses with strong feet and hooves survived. Those who had inferior feet did not endure over the centuries.

Horses can get heat stroke, but they have ways to cool off. They will stand up to their bellies in the breakers of the surf, relaxing in the coldness of ocean water and the relief of the breeze. Beachgoers are always thrilled to see them and gather to take photos and videos. Horses seek reprieve from the sun under beach houses built on pilings. They will lounge under a house for hours, leaving piles of manure as a thank-you.

After the onset of COVID-19, Puckett noticed fewer horses coming to the beach. She believed they were avoiding the growing crowds. During the pandemic, people flocked to the Outer Banks looking for remote, wide-open spaces in wild horse habitat. Realtors and shop owners reported seeing more people than ever in 2020 and 2021. The crowds continued well into the fall and holiday seasons.[106] The horses tended to avoid the crowds, even risking a variation from their normal routine. Still, they can be very visible in their most private moments. A mother horse will carry her foal for about a year before giving birth, usually in a remote place, but not always.

Mares have been known to deliver foals near a house, as in July 2021, when a visitor found afterbirth in the driveway. It was reported to the fund. Herd managers shared photos of the afterbirth with a veterinarian, who said it looked healthy. The new colt turned up the next day robust and energetic.[107] Foals will nurse and stay close to their mothers for as long as two years. The babies sleep a lot and frequently lie on the ground, prompting calls to herd managers from concerned people. Usually, other members of the herd are close by, and the foal is fine.

Chapter 10

ADOPT A HORSE

I n May 2002, for the first time, the fund offered colts for adoption.[108] The buyers would take ownership of the horses and remove them from the beach to a new home. Once again, Little Red Man was the attraction. He had sired all four of the first adopted colts while living at his new home at Dews Island.

Buyers had to complete an application stipulating their ability to take good care of the colts and that they had the facilities and pasture where they could live well. Purchase price for a young horse was $600.[109] The four colts were gelded, vaccinated and examined by a veterinarian and corralled for viewing outside the Cotton Gin, a clothing and gift store in Jarvisburg on U.S. 158. Corolla wild horses sold quickly, displaying the same characteristics that made them good mounts for Spanish explorers. They were good natured, sturdy and intelligent. Each location was visited to make sure the facilities and new owners could properly care for the horse.

In five years, thirty-three stallions were adopted.[110] Herd managers were trying to reduce the number of males. It was better to have several mares per stallion for the welfare of the herd. It also prevented too many lone stallions and reduced fighting. Corolla horses could be one of the rarest breeds in America, said Steve Edwards, owner of Mill Swamp Indian Horses, located in Smithfield, Virginia. Edwards runs a farm where he helps troubled youth and trains wild horses, including those adopted from the Corolla herd. The horses serve as great companions to help the youth overcome problems and learn to love and care for something other than themselves.

A girl rides a tame Corolla horse. *Meg Puckett.*

One of the most famous of those adopted from the Corolla herd is Tradewind. The small stallion weighed a little over six hundred pounds and stood only 12.5 hands when Edwards adopted him in 2009.[111] Tradewind suffered from founder, a condition where soft tissues in the foot are inflamed and damaged, causing severe pain. When he was captured from the wild by McCalpin and Rogers, his hooves were long and curved. His tendons and ligaments were strained, and he had displaced coffin bones (the last bone in a horse's leg, comparable to a fingertip). The hoof forms around this bone.

Tradewind was crippled and was skittish around people.[112] Edwards and others spent months treating the condition until the horse could walk comfortably again. Gradually, the stallion adapted to the saddle and riders. His legs strengthened until he was able to walk and canter for miles at a time with a rider. He became so strong that Edwards entered him into the 2011 National Pleasure Trail Horse of the Year contest run by the Horse of the Americas Registry.[113] Tradewind won the prestigious award for his perseverance and endurance. The "super horse" had traveled 206 hours over the previous year through wooded trails with riders, including Edwards, who weighed over two hundred pounds. Tradewind trotted more than fifty miles on some days. Edwards learned that Corolla wild horses can carry more than 20 percent of their body weight, defying a customary rule. The little mustang still carries riders and sires foals that carry on the Corolla wild mustang bloodlines. Tradewind has become a beacon of overcoming the odds for the troubled youths who come to Edwards's farm. The horse could have been euthanized. Instead, he and his trainers persevered.

Edwards wrote about Tradewind's influence:

> *When I tell teenagers who are fighting to stay clear of drugs what he has overcome, when I tell young adults who suffered molestation as kids what he has overcome, when I tell people whose neurotic parents raised them to hate themselves what he has overcome, when I tell people gripped in clinical depression what he has overcome—that is when he shows his value. That is when he shows his worth.*[114]

Edwards's farm also raises, trains and preserves horse strains such as the Marsh Tacky, Shackleford, Grand Canyon, Brislawn, Galiceno and Choctaw. It is one of the largest and most diverse herds of horses with Spanish heritage in the world.

Tradewind from the Corolla wild horse herd became a champion riding horse. *Sherry Leonard.*

Tradewind left Mill Swamp in 2021 for a farm in Gates County owned by Sherry Leonard. She and a daughter cared for him at Mill Swamp and fell in love with him there.[115] He spends happy days there, Leonard said. He has a gelding friend to keep him company and gets bodywork and chiropractic treatment to keep him feeling well. He gets a special diet to keep him from foundering, the condition that brought about his removal from the wild. He remains a stallion.

"I couldn't bring myself to geld him," Leonard said. "I look at his beautiful face and into his eyes and get the feeling he has lived a thousand lives, and I am compelled to make the rest of this one as pleasant for him as I can."

The fund still manages an adoption program for wild horses removed from the beach. Two of the twenty-two horses living at the farm in 2022 are up for adoption. They are healthy and have no medical issues.[116] Potential owners still have to fill out a form ensuring they have the ability and property to care for the horse. They will also have to spend many hours training with fund staff. The new owner must have barns, a proper feeding and watering program and list how many horses they currently own, among several other qualifications. They must be willing to provide a full-body photograph of the Corolla horse upon request at any time. It's a rigorous process on purpose. Even so, five horses have been returned to the fund in the last six years.

Chapter 11

READY TO RUMBLE

The herd of about 105 horses naturally separates into harems averaging 4 or 5 individuals protected by a stallion, guarding them from a variety of dangers, including challenges from other stallions. Typically, an alpha mare leads the movements of the group, with the stallion following behind watching for danger or challengers. Bachelor stallions hang out together, a normal behavior, but they would prefer to mate and have a harem. They learn how to defend a harem by fighting each other.

Rocky was one those lone stallions for a few years. He had his battles like the boxer that was his namesake. Over time, he fought and often lost as he matured. Eventually, he won some clashes, acquired his own harem and sired foals after his conquest.[117]

Fights can get vicious. Two stallions rise up on their hind legs and kick with their front legs. A favorite move is to bite and hold the withers with an effort to pull down the adversary. Teeth find their mark almost anywhere, ripping whatever they grab. In one recent fight, two horses fiercely battled each other. They dodged each other's attacks for a while before the dominant stallion was able to get a bite on the withers, yank downward and pull his opponent to his front knees. The victim was able to break free but was no longer up for a fight. He instinctively walked into the surf and squatted, allowing the salt water to wash his wounds.[118] Stallions have parts of ears missing, damaged eyes and scars on their bodies from old encounters. They fight often but rarely kill each other. There have been no reports or social media posts in at least twenty-five years of one Corolla stallion killing another.

Stallions fight on the beach. *Meg Puckett.*

The winning stallion will chase his opponent along the beach at full speed with manes and tails flowing. It's a beautiful sight but at the same time dangerous for anyone in the way. They are focused on the fight and have little regard for their surroundings, including traffic or sunbathers. Star, the famous stallion of the 1980s, was a victim of his own rage when he focused only on his challenger and did not see the vehicle in his path.

A man mowing his grass was interrupted by a fight between two stallions that began suddenly in his yard. They battled each other for a while, unaware of any humans nearby and not worried about what or who they ran over. Sand sprayed under their active hooves as they maneuvered for a better position. The man wisely turned off his lawnmower and got out of the way until the battle went elsewhere. He was able to record it on his phone from a safe distance and posted scenes of the encounter on social media.[119]

A horse appropriately named Scar currently roams the banks. His coat demonstrates his long fighting history. He got his name from the many lacerations on his back and legs that healed over and can be seen from the streaks of white hair growing several inches long where each wound was inflicted. They appear in strong contrast to his brown coat like badges of honor in victory or, maybe in some cases, defeat.[120]

At times, challengers use psychological warfare. In the winter of 2019, a young stallion named Moony took on an aging warrior named Topnotch with a different approach. Perhaps he somehow sensed he could not win a one-on-one battle. Maybe he did not want to risk a bad injury. Either way, he decided to try a different tactic. The young horse followed Topnotch and his harem at a distance through a couple of cold months. The veteran kept moving his herd away from the challenger rather than take him on. The older horse looked less and less healthy as his stress increased. The young challenger lurked week after week. Finally, Topnotch could not take it any longer and just walked away, relinquishing his harem without a fight. It appeared he was not up for the confrontation. Maybe, somehow, he knew he would not win. Moony took over the herd without a scratch. In

Top: Stallions fight without a care that a vehicle is close by. *Erin Millar.*

Bottom: One stallion chases another on the beach. *Erin Millar.*

April 2020, the sickly Topnotch was seen alone before he disappeared into the remote marshes. Herd managers thought he might have gone there to die. But he turned up again in May, still alone but much beefier and with a shiny coat. He seemed stress free and healthy again.[121]

Chapter 12

A Refuge for Ailing

and Wayward Horses

I n 2014, the Corolla Wild Horse Fund began leasing a thirty-one-acre tract located on the Currituck mainland just off U.S. 158. Four years later, the fund bought the tract for $550,000. They called it the Betsy Dowdy Equine Center after the girl who rode a wild horse to warn Revolutionary War troops of a British threat to northeastern North Carolina. Karen McCalpin and her staff had searched for a well-suited, convenient farm with plenty of pasture and suitable barns and stables where wayward or sickly wild horses could live out their lives. A property owner in Grandy, on the Currituck County mainland, offered a good deal on a farm.

The fund's options had been limited until then. Little Red Man and his harem were taken to Dews Island in 1999 as they continued to find ways around the fence and cause trouble in Corolla. Dews Island is a private tract located in the Currituck Sound just offshore from Jarvisburg that was the only place available at the time for a few wayward wild horses. The property was not suitable for any more than a few horses, did not have proper facilities for equine care and was not easily accessible by herd managers. Later, the fund sent horses to Steve Edwards at Mill Swamp Indian Horses, but it was far away.

The Grandy farm has become a valuable sanctuary for Corolla wild horses too sick or hurt badly enough that they can no longer stay on the Banks. Some of its residents were and still are horses that repeatedly breached the fence, endangering the harem and causing a hazard in the tourist-filled village. The resident horses can graze in pastures enclosed by white wooden

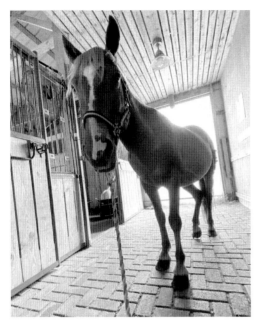

Left: A horse named Junior gets treatment in the barn at the Grandy farm for Corolla wild horses. *Meg Puckett.*

Below: Meg Puckett and a veterinarian care for a horse at the Grandy farm. *Meg Puckett.*

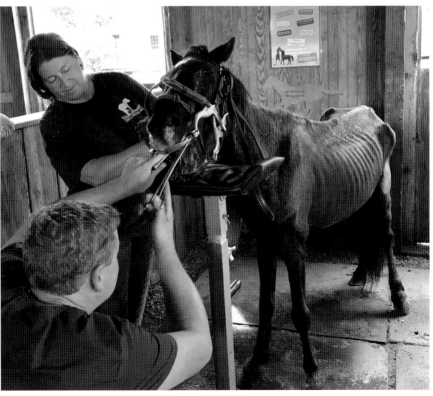

Horses from the Corolla beach now get plenty of hay at the Grandy farm. *Meg Puckett.*

fences. Eight barns provide plenty of housing for the ten or twenty horses typically staying there. What once was a family home with a big front porch serves as an office.

Puckett and her assistant, Nora Tarpley, work daily with the horses to get them accustomed to being around people. The horses get vaccinated, groomed and fed hay. They get used to being led, riding in a trailer and wearing a bridle and a saddle. Each one adapts differently. Some of the horses help with the upkeep by raising money with their own special talents, such as paintings done with a few swishes of a brush attached to their halter. The paintings turn out to be beautiful blends of brush strokes.

Stallions are not gelded. Their rare genes are much too valuable.[122] The farm has a seven-acre woods that covers the backside of the property away from the pastures. Open areas among the trees serve as a burial site for horses. The animals are vaccinated and groomed in the main barn. Keeping them company are a few guinea hens that gobble insects around the property. Horses decide if they want to seek shelter in the barn during cold or stormy weather. In the wild, the mustangs were accustomed to standing under live oak canopies or hiding in thick underbrush.

Taking a horse out of its beach habitat and moving it to the farm is not an easy decision. Herd managers and the board thoroughly weigh the decision. The animal must be suffering from a very serious injury or sickness. Typically, herd managers allow an aging horse to live out its life in the wild. Once the horses have been treated and handled by people, they cannot return to the Outer Banks. Wild mustangs are not vaccinated, and domestic horses are not allowed on the northern banks over fears they may transmit diseases. Wild horses do not miss their old home on the Banks. They adjust to domestic life quickly, enjoying the readily available pasture grass and hay. "A healthy, enriched horse is not standing in the field longing for its days in the wild," Puckett said.[123]

In 2020, the remaining horses on Dews Island were taken to the farm, located just a few miles away, to live out their days. Among them is Moxie, also known as Chaos. She is a mare that goes back to the days of Star and was part of Little Red Man's harem. She was taken to Dews Island with him years ago. Moxie was at least thirty years old as of 2020. In her heyday, she mated with Little Red Man and produced foals on Dews Island such as Little

A couple of horses relaxing in the pasture at the Grandy farm. *Meg Puckett.*

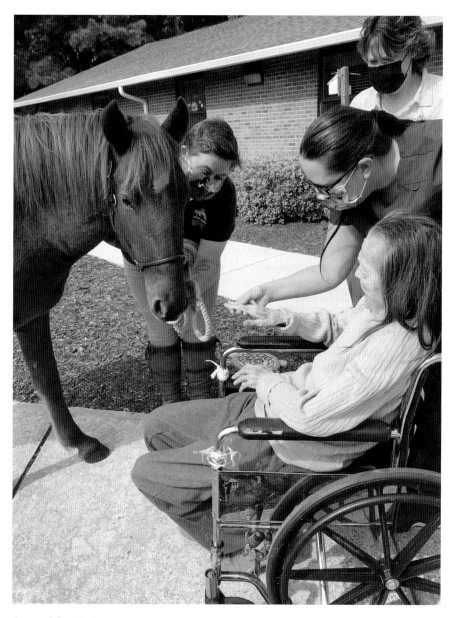

A tamed Corolla horse visits a nursing home with herd manager Meg Puckett. *Meg Puckett.*

Star, Utter Chaos and Bella, which were moved to the farm with her.[124] Each Wednesday from May to September, "Mustang Mornings" is held at the site, where hundreds of visitors come to see and touch a Corolla mustang. Tamed horses are gentle and are taken for visits to public sites such as schools and nursing homes.

A group of horses called the Renegade Six was transferred to the farm in 2018 after repeatedly traveling around the sound side of the fence close to the Virginia line. Led by Lucky Duck, the harem—Virginia Dare, Mateo, Bonita, Ocean Pearl and Kitty Hawk—loved the green grasses found in False Cape State Park. They had the potential of going farther north into the Sandbridge neighborhood, where they could have had dangerous interactions with people and vehicles.[125] The northern fence fell short of the sound, and horses could go around it through the marsh. The fund contracted a company to extend the fence 1,600 more feet into the sound. No matter how many times the Renegade Six traveled north and were brought back to Currituck, they kept escaping into Virginia. One time, rescuers captured them and carried them as far south as possible to an area near Corolla. It did not matter. The pesky harem traveled northward again eleven miles up the beach and over the Virginia border. This time, fund officials relented and brought the six to the farm. Puckett maintained that the young stallion Lucky Duck was obsessive about keeping his harem. He seemed to know he would face less competition from other stallions north of the Virginia fence. Plus, there was the nice green grass.

Chapter 13

IT'S ALL IN THE GENES

I n 2014, a foal named Vivo was born with a defect that caused his leg tendons to contract, forcing him to tiptoe on his hoofs. He was injected with muscle-relaxing medicine, which resolved the condition. He would have died if left on his own in the wild. A report from *The Virginian-Pilot* described the colt afterward:

> *The leggy Corolla colt with a white star on his forehead cautiously followed his mother into the pasture. He pawed the ground and sniffed the new green grass. His fuzzy ears rotated back and forth. Suddenly, he bolted down the white fence line at full speed, stopped at the end and returned galloping, his tiny hoofs flicking dirt behind him. He circled his mother, kicked up his back legs and ran again.*[126]

It was the first time he had scampered and pranced like a wild horse in the month since he was born. The colt was given the name Vivo, Spanish for "I live." Vivo was removed from the herd and taken to the Grandy farm after the extensive human handling. Three other horses had been born with defects in the two previous years, one so severely affected it had to be euthanized. Since then, deformities have been rare.

Part of the problem could have been poor health or nutrition for the mares instead of genetic problems, Puckett said. At the time, the herd numbered 101 horses. The concerns over the deformities brought about another history-making undertaking. A wild horse from the Shackleford Banks herd

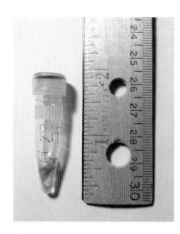

Skin and hair in this tube taken from a Corolla wild horse will provide DNA and help determine heredity. *Author's collection.*

was imported to Corolla with the purpose of expanding the gene pool. The Corolla mustangs descend from a single maternal line, which leads to a lack of genetic diversity.[127] The Shackleford herd of about 110 horses has three maternal lines and lives on three thousand acres largely without human intervention, similar to the Corolla herd. Shackleford Banks is the southernmost barrier island in North Carolina, about nine miles long, and is located in Cape Lookout National Seashore. They called the Shackleford Banks horse Gus after Gus Cothran. To find Gus, a herd manager at Shackleford Banks chose two stallions as candidates. Cothran did DNA tests on them to ensure their genetics were good. One of the horses was found to have a latent gene that could cause blindness. So, Gus was chosen.[128] Years later, unfortunately, Gus still had not sired any foals.[129]

To collect DNA, horses get shot with a dart in the rump that quickly pops out and falls to the ground. It collects a small sample of hair, including the follicle. Hair samples from horses living on the Grandy farm are also collected. The fund is well on its way to getting DNA samples from every wild horse on the north banks. Managers are generating an accurate genealogy so the Corolla wild horses can be recognized as a separate breed.[130]

So far, the fund has established ties back to the 1970s. DNA samples show more than ancestry; they also show behavior patterns and genetic health tendencies. Herd managers can manage contraception to fit DNA profiles that indicate genetic flaws. Amadeo was blind in both eyes, presumably from fights with other stallions. But DNA helped herd managers discover that other horses closely related to Amadeo also had eye defects. They wondered if there was a genetic flaw at work. Skin samples were sent to UC–Davis for specific testing of eye defects in Amadeo's line. Researchers did not find any problems, showing the stallion's blindness was not a genetic defect—good news for the herd.[131] DNA testing has shown a higher tendency for inbreeding among the Corolla herd that live in the more isolated Carova Beach area. It has not proven harmful yet, but it is something the fund is keeping an eye on.

DNA allows herd managers to track breeding behavior and migration on the beaches. They can better deduce the ages of the horses. "The DNA has

A wild horse stands alone on a dune. *Meg Puckett.*

given us a new way to cope with loss," Puckett said. "Amadeo and Roamer may be gone, but their son and grandson share a field at our rescue farm. Taco died prematurely, but we know that he still has brothers and sisters on the beach who can pass his genetics on. Star, the famous stallion who was tragically hit and killed on Highway 12 in the 1990s, has great-grandchildren still living wild and free on the beach today."

Horses gather in the surf often to get away from biting flies swarming in the maritime forests. *Erin Millar.*

Herd managers will make a family tree of stallions and mares that connects to one done in the 1990s. Volunteers at the time wrote that family chain from observation and knowledge of which foal was born to a known stallion and mare. That history began with Star and his mare Baygirl producing a foal named Butterscotch in 1981. Star mated with different mares, producing several offspring, including his son Midnight. One of the keys to bridge the bloodlines is the late stallion Amadeo, which died on the Grandy farm in 2020. His DNA is one of the earliest samples the fund has. He was part of the herd when the Corolla Wild Horse Fund was in its beginnings and is considered a foundation horse. Recent DNA results yielded surprises. Genetic sampling in 2021 uncovered that Raymond's mother was the aging mare Gwen.[132] She was the capricious horse that chose to mate with a donkey living on the Banks. DNA from a mare named Betty indicated she was the daughter of a wild stallion named Captain that lived near the Virginia line, far north of Corolla. Yet she was found living on Dews Island with horses that were once part of the harem of Little Red Man. His harem lived near Corolla. Managers are not sure how she was mixed with Little Red Man's group and taken to Dews Island.

Chapter 14

AMADEO

O n May 2, 2013, two stallions were fighting over mares and territory, a frequent occurrence on the Banks. Except this one involving the blind horse named Amadeo concluded in a way never seen before. He was already blind in one eye. In the fight, his other eye was injured, rendering him sightless in both eyes, and the horse panicked.

He ran from his challenger into the ocean, where he was caught by a rip current that carried him outward and down the beach for more than a mile. He managed to find his footing on a sandbar but froze there, unable to move. He could not see how to get back to the beach as the tide rose, and he faced the threat of drowning. A rescue crew responded after receiving a distress call from a witness. They were not sure at first how to carry out this unusual task. This was a wild animal of about one thousand pounds. Swimmers could not hook an arm around him and pull him ashore with a single flotation device. They called herd manager Wesley Stallings for guidance. Meanwhile, the tide was rising around the horse, and he was becoming more and more anxious. After brief deliberation, the lifeguards retrieved a tow strap from a vehicle and looped it around Amadeo's backside. Then they attached lifesaving buoys. Rescuers connected the strap to a personal watercraft. Slowly, they pulled and guided the stallion toward the shore. He hesitantly followed their lead and soon was walking on the sandy beach. It was the first known rescue of a horse from the ocean by lifeguards, at least on the Outer Banks.[133] The blinded horse could no

Left: The blind horse Amadeo stands in front of a sign at the horse farm in Grandy. *Meg Puckett.*

Right: A girl stands with Amadeo at the Grandy farm. *Meg Puckett.*

longer survive in the wild, prompting herd managers to remove him from his natural habitat. He would live out his days in a safe environment on the Grandy farm set aside for domesticated wild horses. He was christened with the name Amadeo, an Italian term meaning loved or blessed by God. It was a miracle he was alive. Amadeo went from a wild fighting stallion to a docile, much beloved horse that frequently entertained visitors in his later years and even became known as a painter.

He was aided in his artistry, but he appeared to have a flair for it. A brush dipped in paint was fastened to his halter and a piece of paper held to his nose. He seemed to sense his moment and would swipe a few times, creating a painting of flowing brush strokes. The natural, somewhat wild-looking style was a good money raiser for the Corolla Wild Horse Fund.

Amadeo had lived a long life when, late one evening in March 2020, he was unable to stand. Puckett was aware of his declining health and placed a camera in his stall that fed to a screen at home, where she watched his movements.

She noticed on the camera that March evening that he was lying down and trying to crawl his way outside, as if he wanted to be in open air, free from walls in his last breaths, Puckett remembered. She drove to the farm and knelt down by the ailing horse. He did not last much longer. She held his head in her lap as he passed away, tears running down her cheeks. Amadeo was buried in the pasture where he had spent the last few years of his life. His burial spot has remained bare of grass even in the fertile grounds. It's as if the pasture itself honors his last resting place.[134]

Chapter 15

ROAMER

In January 2016, a stallion began appearing regularly in the Villages at Ocean Hill neighborhood of Corolla, which butts up against the Currituck Banks Estuarine Reserve and is close to the fence that blocked horses from coming into the community. Most of the time.

He would be the first significant wild horse challenge faced by Meg Puckett and the last by Karen McCalpin. The stallion would soon earn the much-deserved name of Roamer. The stallion was aging and was not a dominant stallion anymore. He had a dark brown coat, a white patch on his forehead and a black mane and tail. In his prime, he liked blonds, chestnut mares with light-colored manes, and sired many foals. But his days of taking on challengers to his harem were done. He had no more desire to fight stallions and manage mares and foals. He felt more comfortable on the Corolla side of the fence, away from all that drama. McCalpin called him a "happy bachelor." McCalpin lived in that neighborhood. The fence runs along the back side of the homes at the edge of the woods, separating the private property from the Currituck Banks Reserve. McCalpin had dealt with horses coming into Corolla on many occasions because a gate was left open or the fence was in disrepair in a spot. It was no accident or fence malfunction that prompted this horse. He knew how to walk around the end of the fence on the sound to get to the lawns along Lost Lake Lane. Day after day, McCalpin received calls about the horse in her neighborhood. Dispatchers reported this stray horse to her so often that they gave him the name of Roamer. The fund extended the fence farther into the sound and

A horse named Roamer runs along the beach. *Corolla Wild Horse Fund.*

ran a string of electric wire along it. When people approached Roamer to chase him to the other side of the fence, he retreated into the marsh, where it was nearly impossible to reach him. Water moccasins were common in this habitat. He seemed to know the people after him did not want to take the chance of running into a snake.

Over the months, he wandered farther. During the day, he would graze lawns or the Currituck County's sewer treatment plant spray field. Roamer would stand in the shower of the effluent while he continued to eat the lush grass. The smell did not bother him. Visitors renting homes there loved to see him. People standing high on platforms at Corolla Adventure Park were thrilled to see him grazing not far away. In the evening, he would leave that area to get away from coyotes that stalked him at night. He crossed NC 12 to where it was more populated with people and houses and the coyotes were less likely to follow. But it was dangerous to cross the highway. That's why the horses were moved to the north beach in the first place more than twenty years earlier. Roamer followed a strict routine of crossing NC 12 at dawn and returning to the Lost Lake Lane area at dusk. He was so predictable that the fund posted guards on the road to stop traffic when he crossed, according to Puckett. Roamer was the first wild horse the newly hired Puckett had to deal with. She was assigned to go to Lost Lake Lane one day to try to herd him back to the other side of the fence. She drove a fund SUV to the cul-de-sac at the end of the road, and there he stood on the vacant lot. She got out of the truck to confront him.

"He looked at me, and I looked at him," she recalled.

She said out loud to him, "I don't know what I'm doing, but you cannot be here."

She clapped her hands loudly with no luck. She raised her hands high and walked toward him, and finally, he retreated back into the marsh. Of course, it would not be long before he returned. He evaded capture at least twice after receiving a tranquilizer dart shot by McCalpin herself. On both occasions, she had collected volunteers from the local fire departments and trained them on what to do to encircle Roamer to keep him from getting away until the dart took effect. It did not work. He made it through the circle of volunteers and ran off, metabolizing or absorbing the tranquilizer without going down. Locals began calling McCalpin Annie Oakley for her shooting skills. They tried to bait him into a small corral with water or with food such as tasty hay. He did not fall for it. He had enough food and water outside the trap. The efforts to contain him were made tougher by the presence of visitors who wanted to see him, feed him, throw apples or popcorn at him or photograph him at very close range. Dogs chased him. The summer heat could be unbearable near the marsh, and venomous snakes were always present during the warm months. Meanwhile, McCalpin had contacted zoos to find a better, more powerful but safe tranquilizer. She learned of a drug concoction made up of Butorphanol, Azaperone and Medetomidine known as BAM.

On October 12, 2016, after about ten months of trying to restrict Roamer on the north beach, his last day in the wild finally arrived. It wasn't easy for anybody, according to a description from McCalpin. She and a crew of helpers set out five hundred feet of orange plastic fencing around the perimeter of the area where Roamer hung out. She had recruited four cowboys from South Carolina, accustomed to rounding up horses. The veterinarian was there, as well as the fund staff, sheriff's deputies and volunteers who had been trained for the occasion. They quietly surrounded Roamer so McCalpin could get a good shot off from her CO_2 rifle. Then, one of the riders' horses whinnied, alerting the wily Roamer that something was up. He took off for the woods and marsh of the Currituck Banks Research Reserve. The cowboys attempted to head him off, but it looked like he might get away again. Roamer paused for moment.

"I knew it was now or never," McCalpin said. "It was one of the most difficult shots I'd ever taken and one of the most important."

She could barely see him in the brush and woods. She quickly aimed, fired and struck him in a good spot. He ran, and the riders followed. They found him a few minutes later completely unconscious. Now, they had to get the horse of some eight to nine hundred pounds back to the trailer before he woke up. They all gathered to lift and drag him onto a ten-foot corral panel. Four horses and an all-terrain vehicle pulled the panel along the terrain to the trailer in which he was safely loaded.

Roamer would roam no more but would spend the rest of his days at the Grandy farm. Puckett spent hours during his first day at the farm trying to acclimate him to his new home. She sat near him and read books to him such as *Misty of Chincoteague*. She gradually got him used to being touched and receiving a halter. Over time, he became very easygoing. He was one of the most popular and well known of all the wild horses. His photo was featured on a billboard on U.S. 158, the highway where thousands of people travel to and from the Outer Banks each summer day.

Photos of him were frequently posted on social media. An image of him running down the beach was very popular at the gift shop. He was featured in brochures promoting Currituck Outer Banks tourism, and his name and

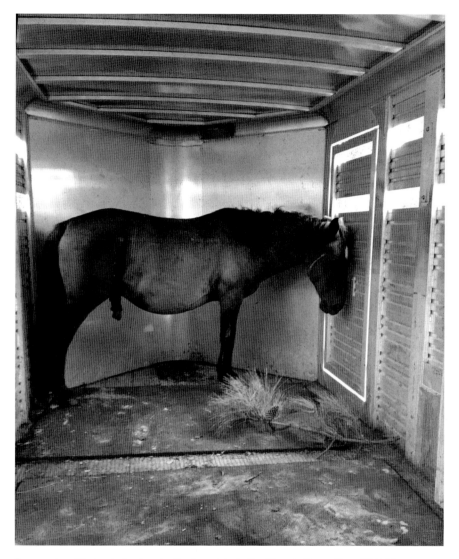

Roamer is safely loaded onto a trailer for a trip to the Grandy farm. *Karen McCalpin.*

photos appeared in books. He was a headliner at the Grandy farm, where the fund held "Meet a Mustang" each week.

He and old Amadeo became good friends, like two old men, Puckett said. She often took him to sites such as the Currituck Beach Lighthouse to meet the public, where he was always so calm and good with children, despite his wild past. When a local water park announced a slide called the Wild Horse, Puckett took Roamer there to be part of receiving a check for a donation to the fund. Puckett loved him as much as she did any horse she's ever owned. She learned how to better handle wild horses when they came to the farm. Typically, domestic horses will raise their foot if a person runs their hand down their leg. Wild horses don't like that sensation and will kick in response. Typically, a stallion challenging another stallion will go for the legs. Puckett learned with Roamer that it was better to tap his hoof or ankle with a stick to get him to lift his foot.

"He taught me so much," she said. "I could be having the worst day, and Roamer could settle me down."

He died in 2019 at more than two decades old.

Chapter 16

RAYMOND THE MULE

One of the famous characters of the horse herd was not a horse; he was a mule named Raymond. He stands only a few hands high, has a dark coat and a mane and tail that have that sun-bleached reddish-blond color, like he was a beach bum. He sort of was in his day. Raymond saw himself as a stallion during his twenty years living among the wild herd. He was feisty and loud, quick to take on a stallion much larger than himself as he attempted to keep possession of his harem of mares. Being a mule, he could not reproduce—not that he didn't try.

Visitors staying in homes in the four-wheel-drive area would report to the fund that they had seen what looked like a mule among the wild horses. They would say it had larger than normal ears and was smaller than most stallions. Some callers would worriedly relate hearing loud, off-key braying that sounded like one of the horses was sick. It was just Raymond.

He devised ways to break through the fence and venture into the Corolla neighborhoods where lush lawns were easy to graze. He was like a magician in the way he could contort his body through a gap in the fence. He could use his head as leverage and break boards, creating a hole large enough to slip through. In large part because of Raymond, Currituck County upgraded the strength of the fence by replacing the two-inch-by-four-inch slats with sturdier two-by-six boards.

After more than twenty years lording over the dunes, Raymond was seen with a bad limp. Over time, herd managers believed he was suffering from chronic lameness in his hoof caused by navicular disease and laminitis. They

Left: Raymond grins for the camera. *Meg Puckett.*

Right: Raymond is a mule that lived among the Corolla wild horses. *Meg Puckett.*

made the difficult decision to move the famous character off the beach in 2019 and over to the mainland farm, where he could live out his days relatively pain free. He was still living like a king in his own stall and pasture as of late 2022.

But wild Raymond did not take well to his new surroundings at first, Puckett remembered. He was brought to the barn at the farm and placed in a stall used to treat ailing horses. The stall is narrower than others and has extra-high walls topped with steel bars for the horses' protection. Raymond was afraid of his new environment and who or what might attack him. He was accustomed to being the little guy that had to constantly defend himself while he was in the wild. He kicked the walls and brayed loudly. He stuck his head into the bars and pried using his body weight so hard it bent the steel frame. Raymond's tantrum lasted two hours as herd managers waited patiently. They knew he was not hurting himself. Finally, he calmed down enough that he could eat his first treats given him by a human. That was a game changer. He seemed to realize he was among friends. His intelligence and personality came through, and he became a favorite of visitors to the farm. People wanted to see Raymond.

One of his favorite treats is marshmallow. When Puckett walked to his pen and called his pet name, Ray Ray, he would run from within his stall and appear from around the wall braying loudly with teeth showing like a big smile. That was the bray people used to hear when he was in the wild and thought it was a sick horse. Raymond is very stubborn and particular. He only eats from his own black bucket that hangs in his stall. It cannot be a different size or color and always has to be in the same place, in the southwest corner of his stall. The bucket must be cleaned from any leftovers from the day before or he won't eat from it. A fan set at the back of the stall keeps the old guy cool in summer. Raymond's aging teeth are so bad his hay has to be the type that comes from what horse owners know as the second cut. Hay crops harvested earlier in the season are the first cut. When the crop grows back and is cut a second time, the hay is more tender and nutritious. Raymond knows the difference and does not eat hay from the first cut. He has come a long way from munching briars and coarse beach grass on the banks. He is in his own little pasture and no longer has to fight for his place against larger foes.

Chapter 17

STILL TRYING TO SAVE HORSES

Wild horse advocates still discover new threats. Herd managers repeatedly warn people against feeding the wild horses carrots or apples like they would a domestic horse. In 2020, a young horse named Danny choked and died torturously after someone gave him an apple. Hundreds of people expressed outrage at the lack of awareness and the boldness of the offender after Puckett posted about the incident on Facebook. Another horse named Junior nearly choked to death on something caught in his esophagus. It passed just in time. It was probably an apple, Puckett said.

Herd managers warn people against feeding the horses in all sorts of ways to better reach more people. They constantly post the warnings on social media, print brochures, speak to people face to face and display the message on large billboards along U.S. 158.

Warmer winters of recent years have allowed pests and bacteria to live longer in the ponds where the horses drink. Three horses died within a year in late 2020 and 2021 after contracting an illness from stagnant water, Puckett said.

A young chestnut horse named Riptide nearly died in 2020 after he was found with a bad wound on his leg just above his foot. He lived near the Virginia line. Riptide had a white patch on his forehead, and people who saw him said he resembled the photogenic and mischievous wild horse Little Red Man.

Wild horses drink from standing water that can contain harmful bacteria. *Corolla Wild Horse Fund.*

A resident reported to the fund that a horse in her yard had a badly bleeding leg. Puckett and others made the long drive up the beach to find Riptide. They assessed how he was doing and took photos for the veterinarian to see. He appeared to be okay, at first. They checked on him for five consecutive days. As his wound became larger, it became necessary to remove him from the beach. It is physically and emotionally difficult to remove a horse from the wild. Herd managers don't do it lightly. Riptide was sent to North Carolina State University, where they could perform surgery and stem the infection. He went through two surgeries. It turned out that the infection was not that deep within the leg, a great indicator that Riptide would survive. He recovered at the university for five weeks before being brought back to the Grandy farm. There, he learned to love hay for the first time and had easy access to a clean bucket of water. The bandage over the wound on his leg was changed every two days. That was the end of his days in the wild, but he was safe, satisfied and healthy, Puckett said. Riptide is popular among visitors to the farm. He even has the reputation of having a goofy personality. He was recently recorded standing in a pasture with a young girl playing ball. The girl rolled a big blue ball to him, and he used his nose to push it back to her. It was not certain who was enjoying the game more, the girl or the horse.

A beautiful black stallion trots along the beach. *Corolla Wild Horse Fund.*

Another horse with a wound similar to that of Riptide had a different result.

A mare named Lizzie developed a wound on her knee in the summer of 2020, not long after giving birth to a colt named Alex, Puckett said. They disappeared for a while in the deep marsh. Even a search in a helicopter did not reveal their whereabouts. Many weeks later, a resident reported seeing Lizzie and Alex in her yard. The colt was strong and healthy, but Lizzie was not doing well. She had a wound like that of Riptide. Again, Puckett and others decided to remove Lizzie from the wild before the wound worsened and infection spread. It was heartbreaking to separate mother and foal, but she would die a horrible death if left on her own in the wild. She was hauled in a trailer down the beach and eventually to the North Carolina State University clinic. The infection was much worse and deeper than that of Riptide. She was operated on and remained in Raleigh to recover for a few weeks. But the wound would not heal; the infection was too deep and had spread. She also developed arthritis in her knee, adding to her pain and inhibiting her ability to walk. Vets and fund managers mutually agreed to euthanize her to relieve her misery. It was a tearful time. Alex was old enough to remain in the wild and as of late 2021 was spotted looking happy and healthy within a new harem. It was later determined that the illness was likely pythiosis, or swamp cancer, caused by fungus-like organisms found in warm ponds and puddles. It can cause lesions to form on the hooves and legs. Once contracted, it must be surgically removed. Medicines are ineffective. Flooding and heavy rains can spread the organism that causes it. The fund recruited "sanctuary observers" who have taken years of detailed notes on the horses they see pretty much daily. The data has been entered onto spreadsheets so that the movement of some horses can be tracked to a precise point of longitude and latitude. The information can be crucial in many ways, such as finding sources of pollution. If a horse dies from drinking contaminated water, for example, the date will show where that horse has been and the most likely spots where it was drinking water. Herd managers could then take water samples and find out where the pollution is and possibly where it originated from.

A mare named Bonita was diagnosed and treated for Lyme disease, another example of an unexpected hazard. Two mares died within a quarter mile of each other after contracting Potomac horse fever, a disease caused by insects such as mayfly larvae living in the horses' drinking water. The second of the two horses to die was taken to the lab in Raleigh for a necropsy, where they confirmed it died from Potomac horse fever. The vet was confident the first mare died from the same thing given the location and circumstances, Puckett said. Potomac horse fever causes diarrhea, fever and mild depression. Cases have been very rare in this region, and as far as anyone knows, no Corolla wild horse had ever died from it before. Cold winters help kill off insects like the mayfly larvae that breed in stagnant water. The fund tested the water and found a significant amount of e. coli in the marshes and ponds, which is normal in water not flushed by the tides or wind currents. Stagnant ponds are the worst places for fever-causing insects.

A beloved eight-year-old stallion named Taco died in October 2021 from drinking contaminated water, according to Puckett. The horse was well known by a large but harmless lump on his hip. It was a sterile abscess that was monitored regularly. A vet said it had nothing to do with his death. He was the third horse in two years to die from drinking contaminated water. It's another potentially fatal problem herd managers are dealing with. They hope for more deep freezes in the winter to kill off deadly organisms. Herd managers were anticipating Taco would produce offspring soon. He had taken a large group of mares from another stallion.

"Every single loss is a tragedy when you have such a small population to begin with, but some hit a bit harder than others," Puckett said. "Taco had such a big personality, and so many people became attached to him and helped us keep a constant eye on him. It's hard to believe he's gone."

A stallion named Hurricane died of heatstroke in 2021 after getting tangled in barbed wire left in a coil on private north banks property. He tried to work himself free for several hours under an intense summer sun. Workers for Dominion Power found the horse in trouble and reported it to the wild horse fund. He was helped free from the wire and seemed fine. A wound on his leg was not serious. Hurricane got up on his feet and went to the beach before collapsing. He could not raise his head and was obviously not recovering. Puckett and others loaded the horse on a trailer and took him to the farm in Grandy, where a veterinarian tried to revive him with intravenous fluids, but it was no use. His organs were failing, and he was euthanized. Puckett posted the incident on Facebook, and it was widely reported in the media. Thousands commented. Afterward, the Corolla Wild Horse Fund put out a notice that loose wire, loose rope, fencing in disrepair, rusted and broken car and boat parts are hazardous to the herd. They should be cleaned up if not being used, the post said.

Overflowing garbage in trash cans near rental homes has also been a horse hazard. A stallion named Arrow became aggressive after pulling bread from a trash container at a home in the four-wheel-drive area. Wild horses can get accustomed to eating scraps in the garbage and get sick. Arrow became a nuisance, scattering the trash and endangering himself and anyone trying to stop him. Puckett attempted to get the bread away from him, and he kicked at her. One person threatened to pour deadly antifreeze into the trash to stop the garbage raids. The fund sent a letter to the homeowners asking them to better enclose their trash containers. More trash cans were placed at the rental homes to better keep the garbage contained. Those steps helped. DNA samples show that Arrow is closely related to Moxie, who was a daughter of Little Red Man, notorious for getting into garbage before being taken to Dews Island. Arrow might have been part of that group years ago. "That might be why he likes garbage so much," Puckett said.

Puckett and assistant Nora Tarpley, like the managers before them, will go to great lengths to save a single horse. Puckett has not taken a vacation in the six years she has worked at the fund. They will spend a night or an entire weekend nursing a sick horse or transporting it to veterinarians at North Carolina State University in Raleigh.

Puckett has mounted two observation cameras at the Grandy farm to keep watch on sickly or aging horses. If a horse has a threatening condition, she sets an alarm to go off hourly so she can check on the animal's well-being.

Generally, the herd is healthy in their harsh Outer Banks habitat. They survived for hundreds of years without human help. Now, with the throng of people mingling among them, they need assistance from those who watch over them.

Success stories help buoy the spirits of herd managers and followers of the wild horses. On Saturday, September 18, 2021, a colt named Bravo was born on the northern Currituck County Outer Banks. His life began in the wild, and wild things happened to him within hours of his birth. His mother, Cora Mae, was fully pregnant, described as "about to pop" when she was last seen on a Saturday morning by Puckett. She gave birth later that day. Early the next day, Puckett checked on the mother and was unable to find the newborn. She drove her aging four-wheel-drive truck back and forth along the sandy roads of Carova Beach for three hours.

Thickets of wax myrtles, reeds and briers grow by the roadsides, offering plenty of cover. Vacant homes offered hiding places among the sheds and shrubbery. He could have been anywhere. Cora Mae was with her harem and looked healthy and normal. Maybe the colt had died early on and its body was left somewhere in the brush. Puckett had searched everywhere she could and returned home sad that the ninth foal born that year may not have made it. Not long afterward, she got word of a sighting from a horse tour guide. She told Puckett of her excitement and how thrilled her customers were to see the new foal, Bravo. The agent was unaware that Bravo had been missing.

Bravo was standing under a vacant house with two other grown horses, she reported. Puckett was ecstatic to hear the good news. She immediately got back into her truck and drove the roughly ten miles from the end of the pavement on NC 12, over the dunes and into Carova Beach, where she found Bravo. She grabbed the tiny black colt in her arms, loaded him into the back seat of her truck and rumbled over a few sand roads past a couple of man-made canals to where his mother was. The experienced mare readily accepted her colt, and the baby began nursing right away. He would have died without her. He was hanging out with Gus and Taka, two horses that typically stayed together. Taka would not have nursed him, but at least she could watch over him temporarily. All was well again.

Puckett guessed that Bravo's father, Nobel, had scattered the mares and Bravo when he charged and fought a challenging stallion. Bravo and his

Wild horses stand along a sunny beach. *Drew Wilson.*

mother became separated and drifted far enough apart that they could not hear or smell each other. Bravo's story is representative of the wild horses and their interactions with humans over the last nearly forty years. It was a natural reaction for a stallion to fight off a challenger and the herd to scatter in the melee. Homes and man-made canals in part prevented Bravo from reuniting with his mother. Yet it was people who cared about him that saved his life.

Bravo the colt became well known to the public after an account of his survival adventure was posted on social media. How will Bravo's life go? Will new dangers find him as they have other wild horses? Will he adapt, or will he need help as he did at the beginning of his life?

History indicates Corolla's wild horses will adapt no matter what the challenges.

Chapter 18

RAISING MONEY

T he fund received a $10,000 grant in 2013 from the Wild Horse Winery and Vineyards in California, one of the largest ever received from a corporate sponsor. The money went largely to help with medical costs of the wild horses.[135] The fund's annual budget at the time was $541,000, covered by donations, grants, gift shop revenues and contributions from Currituck County.

Currituck County granted $50,000 annually to the budget after the fund became a nonprofit. The amount has since grown to more than $69,200 a year as of 2021.[136] The fund's yearly budget grew to $750,000, and membership grew to more than ten thousand by 2020.[137]

Fundraising efforts produce a large portion of the budget. People can become members of the fund with donations as low as $25. Donors can sponsor an individual horse for $75 and receive an embossed leatherette folder with a photo and information about the horse's life. Tributes in someone's memory or to honor someone's birthday or wedding anniversary begin at $50. Property owners can pledge $20 for each of the thirteen weeks of prime tourist season for a total of $260. The fund also takes donations through a will or a life insurance policy. Land donations in the four-wheel-drive area are welcomed. Local landowner Jay Bender set aside acreage as part of the horse refuge nearly twenty years ago.

Many have created artwork about the herd, such as resin horsehead ornaments, key chains with horsehair tassels and shell ornaments painted with horse images. These items are available at the Corolla Wild Horse Museum shop on Corolla Village Road.

Clay Pots and Ornaments

In 2019, Mike Middleton of Moyock began making one-of-a-kind pots decorated with Corolla wild horsehair. Middleton teaches pottery at a high school in Chesapeake, Virginia, just on the other side of the state line from his home. The quick-selling pots are made from natural Currituck clay, hearkening back to Native pottery made hundreds of years ago. Middleton shovels about one thousand pounds of clay every two weeks from his neighbor's pasture. The clay then has to dry to eliminate bacteria. Before he can begin the artwork, he adds enough water to make a soupy mix.

Top: A Christmas ornament of pottery made by Mike Middleton is shaped like the head of a Corolla wild horse. *Meg Puckett.*

Bottom: Mike Middleton makes clay pots glazed with hair from wild horses. Part of the proceeds goes to the Corolla Wild Horse Fund. *Author's collection.*

Then he pours it through drop cloths used for painting to separate out the sand. The thick brown muck dries again in a tray. He mixes in talc and clay powder to strengthen it, transforming the concoction into a usable medium. He forms a pot in minutes on his turning wheel. The pot goes into the kiln to be fired at 1,900 degrees. He removes it and lets it cool before applying a glaze. Here is where it becomes a unique piece connected to the Corolla wild horses.

To apply horsehair, he fires the pot again at 1,300 degrees, removes it with tongs and within seconds carefully holds strands of hair close to the pot as it spins slowly on the turning wheel. The heat is so intense it can singe his eyebrows if he is not careful. The horsehair instantly incinerates into a carbon print of what resembles black veins in an unpredictable design as wild as the horses themselves. Each pot is one of a kind. A two-thousand-year-old Native American clay pot on display at the Museum of the Albemarle in Elizabeth City inspired Middleton to work with local "wild clay." His first pot was decorated with hair from the late wild horse named Roamer. Herd managers saved some of his hair before he died. They regularly supply Middleton with hair from various horses and the famous mule Raymond. At one of his first sale events early in 2019, he and his wife set up fifty-three pots for sale on his Moyock property. He advertised on social media, hoping to sell a few over the course of the day. They began at ten o'clock in the morning and watched as crowds showed up. They sold out in about thirty minutes. It was shocking how fast they sold that day. Wild horsehair pots, bowls and jars are on sale at the Corolla Wild Horse Fund store in Corolla and at Middleton's website at michaelmiddletonceramics.com. Prices range from $75 to $120. A percentage goes to the fund.

A CHILDREN'S BOOK

Broken-hearted grandmother Kelley Horton corroborated with local children's book author Brandi McMahan to produce *Sebi the Colt*, the story of a boy who dies and returns as a Corolla wild horse. Horton wrote the book after her nine-year-old grandson, Sebastian "Sebi" Lopez, and his mother, Rayann Horton, thirty-nine, died in a 2020 Kill Devil Hills house fire. They were found in a bedroom holding each other. Horton and McMahan wrote the book to help deal with the pain and perhaps help others who have experienced similar tragedies. Sebastian loved the wild horses and had gone to the Currituck Banks to see them with his mother. After his death, the fund named one of the new colts Sebi in his honor. In the book, Sebi runs free on the beaches with his mother, who has returned as a raven and flies nearby. The proceeds go to the fund and other charities.

A VIDEO

A movie called *The Secret of Corolla: The Gift from the Outer Banks* was produced by Jerry Thompson of Big Dog Films. The cost is fifteen dollars. The film tells the history of the Corolla wild horses and how they have adapted and survived on the Currituck Outer Banks.

A SONG

Kelly Wilkes, a volunteer with the fund, and Janet Martin, a songwriter from Richmond, Virginia, combined to write an original song about the wild horses titled "Castano," based on an actual chestnut stallion living on the Banks. The song, video and lyrics are available at www.corollawildhorses.org as a download for five dollars. Supporters can donate more if they wish. All proceeds go to the Corolla Wild Horse Fund.

Notes

Chapter 1

1. Interview with Dru Hodges, founding member of the Corolla Wild Horse Fund, 2021.
2. Interview with Corolla realtor Kay Cole, 2021.
3. Interview with Hodges.
4. www.corollawildhorses.com.
5. *The Virginian-Pilot,* June 27, 1990, D1.
6. Corolla Wild Horse Fund genealogy chart.
7. *The Virginian-Pilot,* May 14, 1991, D1.
8. Interview with Drew Wilson, 2021.
9. Ibid.
10. Interview with Meg Puckett, 2022.

Chapter 2

11. Robert Denhardt, *The Horse of the Americas* (Norman: University of Oklahoma Press, 1975), 25.
12. www.spanishbard.com.
13. Shackleford-horses.org citing the Archives of the Indies.
14. Daniel Johnson, "Hard Evidence of Ancient American Horses," *BYU Studies Quarterly* 54, no. 3.

15. Denhardt, *Horse of the Americas*, 48.
16. Ibid., 37.
17. Ibid., 41.
18. www.ncedia.org, an online history administered by the State of North Carolina.
19. Shackleford-horses.org.
20. Ibid.
21. Corollawildhorses.com.
22. John Lawson, *A New Voyage to Carolina* (London, 1709), 81.
23. Edmund Ruffin, *Archaeological, Geological and Descriptive Sketches of Lower North Carolina and Similar Adjacent Lands* (Raleigh, NC: Institution for the Deaf, Dumb and Blind, 1861), 131. Made available online by the University of North Carolina at Chapel Hill at docsouth.unc.edu.
24. www.corollawildhorses.com.
25. Equine Preservation Organization, "Horse of the Americas," 2007.
26. www.equus-survival-trust.org.
27. Email from Victoria Tollman to the author, 2022.

Chapter 3

28. Corolla Wild Horse Fund records.
29. Interview with Dru Hodges, 2021.
30. Corolla Wild Horse Fund records.
31. *The Virginian-Pilot*, June 20, 1990, D1.
32. Interview with Hodges.
33. Interview with Kay Cole.
34. Corolla Wild Horse Fund daily journal.
35. *The Virginian-Pilot*, June 12, 1999, B1.
36. Interview with Ernie Bowden, 2019.
37. *The Virginian-Pilot*, August 23, 1993, D1.
38. Ibid.
39. Letter from Corolla Wild Horse Fund to membership, November 1994.
40. *The Virginian-Pilot*, March 29, 1994, D1.
41. *The Virginian-Pilot*, June 30, 1994, B1.
42. *The Virginian-Pilot*, June 22, 1995, B1.
43. *The Virginian-Pilot*, October 24, 2019, A2.
44. *The Virginian-Pilot*, June 22, 1995, B1.
45. Interview with Donna Snow, 2021.

46. *The Virginian-Pilot*, June 19, 1999, B1.
47. Ibid.
48. *The Virginian-Pilot*, June 12, 1999, B1.
49. Ibid.
50. Interview with Meg Puckett, 2021.
51. *The Virginian-Pilot*, July 11, 2001, B1.

Chapter 4

52. Interview with Bob White, 2021.
53. *The Virginian-Pilot*, June 27, 2010, Y1.

Chapter 5

54. Interview with Lloyd Childers, 2021.
55. *The Virginian-Pilot*, January 12, 2000, B1.
56. Ibid.
57. Interview with Puckett.
58. Interview with Karen McCalpin, 2021.
59. Interview with Mike Hoff, 2021.

Chapter 6

60. *The Virginian-Pilot*, December 4, 2001, B1.
61. *The Virginian-Pilot*, February 3, 2002, Y1.
62. *The Virginian-Pilot*, December 29, 2001, A9.
63. *The Virginian-Pilot*, December 6, 2001, B1.
64. Interview with Donna Snow, 2022.

Chapter 7

65. *The Virginian-Pilot*, January 5, 2003, B1.
66. *The Virginian-Pilot*, June 18, 2001, B1.
67. *The Virginian-Pilot*, February 14, 2006, Y1.
68. Interview with Karen McCalpin, 2021; *The Virginian-Pilot*, August 21, 2006, Y1.

69. Ibid.
70. *The Coast,* July 2, 2010, 6.
71. Corolla Wild Horse Fund Facebook page, June 10, 2014.
72. *The Virginian-Pilot,* June 3, 2007, B1.
73. Interview with McCalpin, 2021.
74. Corollawildhorses.com.
75. *The Virginian-Pilot,* June 3, 2007, B1.
76. Ibid.
77. *The Virginian-Pilot,* October 28, 2008, A9.
78. *The Virginian-Pilot,* May 16, 1993, B1.
79. Ibid.
80. *The Virginian-Pilot,* May 28, 2009, B3.
81. Ibid.
82. *The Virginian-Pilot,* October 7, 2009, B7.
83. *The Virginian-Pilot,* July 12, 2009, B4.
84. Wtkr.com.
85. Interview with McCalpin, 2021.
86. *The Virginian-Pilot,* November 22, 2009, B2.
87. Interview with Puckett, 2022.
88. Ibid.
89. Interview with McCalpin, 2021.

Chapter 8

90. Ibid.
91. Ibid.
92. Report of a 2011 legislative hearing in the U.S. Congress before a natural resources subcommittee.
93. Corollawildhorses.com.
94. Ibid.
95. Interview with McCalpin, 2021.
96. Interview with Puckett, 2021.

Chapter 9

97. Corollawildhorses.com.
98. Ibid.
99. Currituck National Wildlife Refuge 2008 Conservation Plan.
100. Currituck County planning department.
101. Ibid.
102. Coastalreview.org, October 29, 2013.
103. Corollawildhorses.com.
104. Ibid.
105. Facebook; Corollawildhorses.org.
106. Interview with Puckett, 2021.
107. Ibid.

Chapter 10

108. *The Virginian-Pilot*, May 8, 2002, B1.
109. Ibid.
110. Interview with Snow, 2021.
111. *The Virginian-Pilot*, January 14, 2012, B1.
112. Interview with Steve Edwards, 2021.
113. Ibid.
114. Email from Steve Edwards and Mill Swamp Indian Horses, October 2021.
115. Interview with Sherry Leonard, 2022.
116. Interview with Puckett, 2022.

Chapter 11

117. Ibid.
118. Corollawildhorses.org Facebook page.
119. Ibid.
120. Interview with Puckett, 2021.
121. Ibid.

Chapter 12

122. Ibid.
123. Ibid.
124. Ibid.
125. Ibid.

Chapter 13

126. *The Virginian-Pilot,* June 22, 2014, A3.
127. *The Virginian-Pilot,* April 16, 2018, A1.
128. Interview with McCalpin.
129. Interview Meg Puckett.
130. Ibid.
131. Ibid.
132. Ibid.

Chapter 14

133. *The Virginian-Pilot,* May 16, 2013, B1.
134. Interview with Puckett.

Chapter 18

135. *The Virginian-Pilot,* May 16, 2013, B1.
136. Currituck County budget.
137. Corolla Wild Horse Fund.

Index

A

Amadeo 32, 91, 92, 93, 94, 95, 96, 101

B

Betsy Dowdy Equine Center 84

C

Childers, Lloyd 9, 39, 47
Cothran, Gus 61, 91
Currituck National Wildlife Refuge 12, 34, 47, 50, 59, 64, 69

D

DNA 28, 61, 91, 93, 110
Dowdy, Betsy 22, 23, 84

E

Edwards, Steve 77, 78, 79, 84

F

fence 34, 35, 36, 37, 38, 42, 47, 55, 62, 84, 89, 90, 97, 99, 103

G

Grandy farm 84, 90, 91, 93, 95, 100, 101, 107, 111

H

Hodges, Dru 9, 14, 16, 29, 35, 47
Horse of the Americas 21, 59, 67, 78

L

Langone, Jo 68
lighthouse 13, 32, 40
Little Red Man 29, 31, 37, 38, 39,
   40, 77, 84, 87, 93, 106, 110

M

McCalpin, Karen 9, 50, 57, 59, 61,
   62, 64, 66, 67, 68, 78, 84, 97,
   99, 100
Monto'ac 52

P

Puckett, Meg 8, 9, 19, 28, 52, 57,
   63, 68, 75, 86, 87, 89, 90, 92,
   95, 97, 99, 100, 101, 104,
   105, 106, 107, 108, 109, 110,
   111

R

Roamer 92, 97, 99, 100, 101, 102,
   114

S

Snow, Donna 9, 37, 39, 41, 47, 53
Snow, Gene 39, 41, 53
Spanish Mustang Registry 24, 25,
   59
Star 11, 13, 16, 17, 18, 19, 20, 29,
   31, 37, 38, 61, 62, 68, 82, 87,
   92, 93

T

Tollman, Victoria 28
tours 42, 45
Tradewind 78, 79, 80

ABOUT THE AUTHOR

J eff Hampton was a reporter for more than thirty years who covered the Outer Banks for *The Virginian-Pilot* newspaper. He wrote more than one hundred stories about the Corolla wild horses. He and his wife live in his native county of Currituck.

Visit us at
www.historypress.com